PRACTICAL
WISDOM ᴼᴿ
SUCCESSFUL
LIVING

GASPAR ANASTASI

▌ Forward

'm so excited to share with you the contents of the following pages—practical wisdom for successful living that the Lord has placed in my heart. In fact, much of what you'll read comes from my personal time with the Lord. I shared these messages originally as blogs on our website: GasparandMichele.com. We decided to put them in print as well so that we could reach as many people as possible. My prayer is that this book will be a tremendous blessing to you as we all walk the journey of life.

I encourage you to use it as a reference book, picking it up again and again as you confront different issues in life. Read the messages, write out then meditate on the scriptures included in them, letting the Word of God seep down deep in your spirit. I encourage you to keep a journal of what the Lord shows you. I trust that these messages will bring much needed direction, guidance, healing and success to your life. God bless you.

Pastor Gaspar Anastasi

Contents

De-stressing Your Life

▌ Improving Your Memory

With all the stress we face today, it seems like people are forgetting more things than ever before. I always hear people complaining about "having a senior moment" or a "brain freeze" when they forget something important. Of course they're alluding to the fact that as we get older, our memory becomes more dysfunctional. I'm sure many of you reading this blog can think of important things you've recently forgotten.

Let me first say that one reason older people are more forgetful than younger people is because they haven't exercised their mind. Like other organs in the body, the brain needs exercise. Today's world gives us access to hundreds of TV channels and our computers and phones think for us and solve our problems. Because we don't exercise our brains, we forget more—a problem not just limited to the "older folks."

Stress is also a factor in diminishing our memory because it makes us poor listeners. If we aren't paying attention because of our stress and busyness, we're going to be more forgetful. I've noticed that when I talk to some people, they can't listen intently because they're too distracted by what's important to them, not me. They just can't wait for me to finish so they can talk. If you asked what I said, they couldn't remember because they didn't really hear me. Jesus talks about this in Mark 4, "….Take heed what you hear. With the same measure you use, it will be measured to you; and to you who hear, more will be given."

Here are a few tips to improve your memory:

Become a good listener. Discipline yourself to value the person talking and show honor and respect to them by listening. Listen with an open mind, believing that what they say is important to you. We shut out the speaker by assuming the information's not important or we think we already know that. Most people can't even remember what the preacher's Sunday message was about if you ask them!

Exercise your brain. The adage, "if you don't use it, you'll lose it" is true with everything in life. Make it a practice to memorize at least one thing every day—preferably the word of God. It will exercise your brain and will feed your spirit. It's difficult in the beginning because you haven't used your memory, but if you're consistent it gets easier.

Read more and cut your TV and computer time. Reading develops your brain's thinking process and ability to remember. Conversely, TV and computers entertain your brain, giving information without the need to comprehend and reason out the information. The memory part of your brain gets lazy. Not all computer time is bad, but because it's so entertaining, it can easily become an addiction.

Challenge yourself to learn new things. Using your brain to do things that are new and out of the ordinary, develops new habit patterns that will stimulate your memory. Things like learning a new language or a new board game like scrabble, forces you to think and have memory recall. Dementia can be avoided in later years if you develop good habits to increase your memory capacity.

Don't allow yourself to be constantly offended. I conclude by saying unforgiveness hardens your heart (spirit mind) and affects your natural mind. When your mind is consumed with unforgiveness and bitterness, you quickly become a forgetful person. It doesn't matter how many vitamins and memory supplements you take, until you forgive and walk in God's love, your memory will keep deteriorating. God gave us a mind to discern His heart.... a mind that's creative... a mind that manifests His greatness in our life and the lives of others.

The battle today is about who controls your mind. Don't give Satan the upper hand in this battle. Make Jesus Lord over your mind by keeping it in good shape!

▐ Living a Stress-Free Life (Part 1)

We live in a world filled with stress and there isn't anyone living on the face of the earth today not affected by it. 43% of all adults (almost half the adult population living on the planet) suffer sickness that can be related to stress.

Even doctors admit that 80% of all sickness is stress-related. And, in America it's reported that one million workers are absent every day because of stress-related issues.

Since most people don't even recognize that they are living under stress, I am listing some of the spiritual, emotional and physical symptoms to look for. I only mention a few because of space limitations.

- Loss of sleep

- Bouts of mood swings and fits of anger

- A desire to run away from it all

- Dry mouth, itching, loss of hair

- Eating disorders

- A lack of a desire for intimacy with God

- Excessive worry

- Feelings of insecurity

Remember that most of our current society deals with stress through medication and on-going psychological counseling. But I would like to give you some simple solutions to the overwhelming problem of stress. Are you ready to live a stress-free life? Okay…..here we go!

1. Get re-acquainted with God. The biggest stress producer is not getting your basic needs met. But, Philippians 4:19 tells you that the one and only true God will (and wants to) supply all your needs. Believe in the one and only true God and get rid of all the other gods.

2. Cast your cares upon Him (1 Peter 5:6&7). The only way to cast all your concerns, worries and anxieties on God is if you actually trust Him as God. If you don't, you will wind up becoming your own god. If you are stressed it's because you are not trusting God for everything in your life.

Humble yourself: Don't make yourself god, but trust Him with all of your needs.

Keep your worries in God's hands, not yours: Check yourself often to see if you took these cares back. If you did, give them back to God again.

3. Satan is the biggest stress-master. He knows that if you aren't walking in a stable place and you are stressed, he can get inside your thoughts, emotions and even your body.

You can live a stress-free life and not fall into the trap of Satan's assignment in your life.

▍ Living a Stress-Free Life (Part 2)

There is so much to cover when it comes to the topic of stress, so I want to add to yesterday's simple steps on how to live a stress-free life. Recognizing a few of the fundamental areas are as follows:

1. God is the source of all our needs...not ourselves...and not other people: Forgetting that in itself causes stress.

2. We must recognize that we are stressed out and also see the root causes of that stress: (For me, at one time it was other people's opinion of me. I was being judged by some concerning my leadership and I was taking it to heart rather than giving it over to God. I wasn't trusting Him to resolve those issues and protect me.)

In today's message, I would like to add to those simple truths by giving you three additional steps that changed my life. I believe it will change yours as well. They are found in Philippians 4:6&7:

3. In everything pray. Prayer is the centerpiece of living a stress-free life and without it there is no hope. Most people live a prayerless life—proof that they haven't accepted God as their source.

4. Make supplication. This means finding the answer to your needs in God's word and then presenting it back to Him as a formal prayer request. God wants us to remind Him of His word. His word won't fail us when we believe Him and hold Him to it. John 15:7

5. Thank Him for meeting your needs. When you live a life of prayer you will also thank Him for His provisions, even before they are manifested in your life. Thanking Him is proof that you trust Him as God. It will release God's peace into your spirit (which is the center of a stress-free life).

In summary, here are all the steps for living a stress-free life:

1. Get re-acquainted with God

2. Humble yourself

3. Cast your cares upon Him

4. Know that Satan is the stress-master

5. In everything pray

6. Make supplication: praying the end from the beginning

7. Thank Him daily for meeting your needs

Breaking Chains of Bondage

▍ Breaking Destructive Life Cycles

We've all developed bad habits in life that we wish we didn't have to keep dealing with. I'm talking about bad habits that have eventually led to destructive cycles. Living with a critical spirit, an unforgiving heart, a poor self-image, gossiping, losing your temper, overeating, being lustful, etc. are all behaviors that set up destructive cycles and patterns. These cycles are detrimental to our success and especially detrimental to our witness as a Christian.

One of the great dangers of not breaking these deadly cycles is that we mistake activity for progress. We convince ourselves that staying busy for the Lord is a sign of our Christian maturity (wrong).

Another danger is, if we try to change but repeatedly fail, and slip back into the same destructive life cycle. There is a tendency to give up trying and instead make excuses and allowances for them. The worse thing we can do is make excuses for wrong attitudes and fleshly appetites and continue on as though we've dealt with them.

I propose a biblical method that God guarantees will break those destructive cycles in your life forever. It's so simple that we excuse it because of its simplicity. In fact many of you reading this are saying to yourself, I know if it's too simple it can't work. You'll stop reading and shut yourself down to God's guaranteed method to break destructive cycles.

We humans like to intellectualize everything and make it complicated, so when we do accomplish them we feel like we have achieved something. God, on the other hand, makes things so simple. He only requires that we have faith in His methods. So, when it's all said and done, He's the one who accomplished something in our lives, not us. He tells us that in Zechariah 4:6b, "Not by might nor by power, but by My Spirit,' Says the LORD of hosts."

Here it is.... are you ready to break the destructive and deadly cycles in your life? Change your speech patterns! We've all heard Proverbs 18:21 many times before, "Death and life are in the power of the tongue, and those who love it will eat its fruit." Well it's true: You are the sum total of all the words you have spoken over your life for years and all the words others have spoken over you, that you believed.

Changing what you say about yourself will eventually cause change in you and set you free from those destructive cycles. Yes, it's really that simple! So, pick one area where a destructive cycle is manifesting and think about what you've been saying that's brought you into agreement with it. If it's self-worth, have you been saying or agreeing with words that put you down, belittle you, call you a failure or a mess up? When anything goes wrong, do you always say it's because of you and nobody else?

After you discover what confessions have contributed to those destructive cycles do the following:

1. Repent to God for demonically inspired words by breaking any agreement with Satan and his plans for your life.

2. Receive God's forgiveness and forgive yourself for saying them and repeating them over your life.

3. Release what God says over you. Seek God's plan for your life and replace Satan's plans by confessing God's word instead. Remember, your mouth speaks what's in the abundance of your heart. Keep filling your heart and mind with God's words, not what your temporary circumstances say.

4. Break the curse of those destructive words you've been confessing over your life. Say, "I break the curse of all the words (name them) I've said that have caused this destructive cycle in my life." And say, "I replace those words with this blessing (God's word) over me. I declare that I'm blessed."

That's it! It's that simple. Oh yes, you must guard your mouth and not speak those negative things again. If you do slip back, quickly repent and repeat the above process again. Within one month's time you will be free from those destructive life's cycles in your life. Try it, God guarantees it.

▮ Breaking False Boundaries

oundaries are limits that were either placed on our lives by r ourselves or by outside forces. They're strongholds in our minds that cause false perceptions of what we can or can't accomplish. They dictate how we can live or how we can't live. They're deceptions in our mind that distort reality and blind us to what's true and what's false. The boundaries around our life keep us away from the success and destiny in Jesus Christ that we were created for.

One of the strongest boundaries that Satan places around us is fear. FEAR: False Evidence Appearing Real! I'm not talking about the natural fear we are born with, the kind of fear that protects us from real danger. But I'm talking about the spirit of fear that paralyzes and blinds us to God's truth. Unfortunately, I see many people so bound up with fear, that their walk with God has been hindered.

2 Timothy 1:7 says, "For God has not given us a spirit of fear, but of power and of love and of a sound mind." This verse tells me that the kind of fear that creates worry, anxiety, phobias, torment, etc., is a direct result of a spirit of fear. We don't have to live that way, yet many have actually accepted fear as a way of life and try to live with it, while others deal with the torment of fear through the use of drugs. Today, prescription pills are the "quick cure" for people who suffer from fear, so it's no wonder we see so many people addicted to prescription drugs.

Take a look at some principles below that I believe will help you break the false boundaries of fear.

1. Recognize that fear is a spirit. You have been given dominion over every demon spirit that attacks you as it says in Luke 10:19, "Behold, I give you the authority to trample on serpents and scorpions, and over all the power of the enemy, and nothing shall by any means hurt you " Aggressively resist that spirit of fear by believing the word of Doctor Jesus. His prescription is the "gospills" (His words) and they aren't addictive or mood altering!

2. Fear creates tremendous insecurity, so get to really know God's love firsthand. Someone else telling you that God loves you is not good enough. Only Gods' love can make your heart trust God's promises for you and your destiny and will cancel out Satan's lies! 1 John 4:18 says, "There is no fear in love; but perfect love casts out fear, because fear involves torment." Knowing the depth of God's love brings security and the strength to resist the False Evidence That Appears Real. Be patient with yourself during this time of learning how much God loves you. Too many of us have fallen into self-hatred and condemnation because we didn't understand this spiritual war.

3. Closely watch the kind of books, TV shows and movies you're watching and listening to. The wrong ones will just intensify your fears. This is war, so be disciplined about what you allow to enter your mind and spirit, because your eyes and ears are the gateways to those areas.

4. Understand the transference of spirits. Who you hang around with is who you become like! Avoid spending time with fear-filled people and remember, like spirits are attracted to each other. It's likely your friends have the same problems you do, so choose new friends who are walking victoriously with God.

Conclusion: Fear can and should be defeated, but if you don't contest it, it will become a full-blown phobia. Don't open the door to a demon-controlled life, limited by false boundaries. If you let

Satan in, he will continue to place more and more limits around you. Remember, Jesus already set you free..... John 8:36, "Therefore if the Son makes you free, you shall be free indeed."

▍Coming Out of the Cave

t doesn't matter how "spiritual" or "together" we may think we are. Every one of us will have at least one cave experience in our lifetime. Even the mighty man of God, the Prophet Elijah, had to go through his cave experience.

Elijah had just won the most amazing victory over the prophets of Baal and turned the children of Israel back to serving and worshiping Yahweh, the true God. God answered Elijah when he called fire down from heaven, making an open show of the false god Baal and those who served him.

Look at what happens next to Elijah in I Kings 19:3, "Then Jezebel sent a messenger to Elijah, saying, "So let the gods do to me, and more also, if I do not make your life as the life of one of them by tomorrow about this time." And when he saw that, he arose and ran for his life, and went to Beersheba, which belongs to Judah, and left his servant there."

As we can see, immediately after this amazing act of boldness and bravery, Elijah was overcome by a spirit of fear from the words of just one woman, Jezebel! He became so fearful from her threat to kill him that this man of many miracles ran away for his life and hid himself in a cave!

Sometimes we also find ourselves in "the cave" after a great success because for every mountain there are two valleys. After a victory sometimes we can feel let down, get really depressed and fearful and even sense that maybe God is not with us anymore. Or can we feel that somehow we blew it!

First Corinthians 10:13 tells us that we all face the same temptations (challenges), that they are common to all humans. This verse also tells us that God always makes a way out for us.

That is why the cave experience is not necessarily a bad thing. God can use it as an opportunity to give us a greater anointing and calling. That's what happened to Elijah. The Lord spoke to him at the cave in a small still voice, assured him that he was not alone in his service to God and gave him his instructions for the rest of his ministry.

Like Elijah, our cave experience can be the turning point of our life. The cave can be a womb, a place of new birth. That place of loneliness, despair; the place where it seems like we are separate from God, can actually become the place where our destiny is birthed!

Or, if we choose to stay in that place of loneliness and despair, only listening to the voice of the devil instead of listening to the voice of God, we will never be set free. Instead of the cave being a womb, the place of new life, it becomes a tomb, a place of death and darkness. It becomes a place where we bury our dreams and hopes and we can even turn away from serving God.

God's about to show us the new anointing He wants to give us. He wants to birth a new vision for our life and tell us how to achieve it. But, He may be allowing circumstances in our life that make us run to the cave, the quiet place so He can meet with us there.

So don't be afraid to run to the cave. That cave experience can be where you find your new beginning, your new life. But like Elijah, seek God in that place, hear Him and then, don't stay there.... Come Out Of The Cave!

▌ The Cure for Loneliness

et me start by saying its untrue that the only people who are lonely are either single or alone. The truth is, I know quite a few married folk who are extremely lonely as well. God created each of us to have an intimate and personal relationship with Him first and then with one another. When that doesn't occur (for whatever reason) it brings emptiness inside our spirit, producing feelings of loneliness.

When we spiritually and emotionally connect to our Creator and other humans, we feel fulfilled and whole and are strengthened to handle our problems with greater success. Lonely people don't handle stress well and are more prone to break down emotionally. And lonely people are more susceptible to depression, suicidal thoughts, sickness, etc.

Here are some things to help cure your loneliness.... whether married or single.

Stop looking to another person as your source of happiness and fulfillment because it sets you up for future rejection and great feelings of loneliness. That's too much pressure for you or anyone else to be put under. Look to God, He's the only one who can give us true fulfillment, joy and happiness in our lives. Yes, He will use other people to accomplish that, but He is the source of life and the antidote for loneliness.... not them. So many married couples suffer severe feelings of loneliness because they look to their spouse for what only God can supply!

Recognize that you're valuable and special as God's creation.... all by yourself. Too many singles feel inferior and worthless and look for value through connecting with anyone who's available, leading to deep emptiness and loneliness. They make poor decisions in their choice of friends and soul mates in their attempt to satisfy the need to feel accepted and valuable. Unfortunately, two wounded and unfulfilled singles don't make a whole relationship....quite the contrary!

So, find your identity in Jesus Christ, knowing that when He made you, He didn't make junk (despite feeling and hearing differently). Connect with His plans for your life by giving Him access to your heart.

That connection comes from reading His word daily and believing what He says about you. Ephesians 3:20, "Now to Him who is able to do exceedingly abundantly above all that we ask or think, according to the power that works in us". The power that works in us comes from believing God's word for our life.

I recommend you read every scripture that tells you who you are in Christ and what you can do in Him. Philippians 4:19, "I can do all things through Jesus Christ who strengthens me".

Take the pressure off those you relying on to fill that void. Release them right now and place your eyes, trust and hope in God. Allow God to use whatever instrument He wills to heal your loneliness.

Take an inventory of your life and count your blessings. Too often we only focus on the negative things. We need to look at WHAT WE DO HAVE instead of WHAT WE DON'T HAVE, so we'll realize how much God loves us and how much He's done for us. In time we will see how valuable we really are to God.

Finally, take dominion over your thought life. Feelings of lone-liness are produced by thoughts about your past, present and future life. Don't give the devil freedom to mess around with your thoughts. He knows that God's word tells us, "As a man thinks in his heart, so shall he be".

Decide today to make Jesus Lord over your thoughts. Every time loneliness overtakes you, stop and realize that its source is what you're thinking. Ask the Holy Spirit to reveal your thoughts to you and, with His help, tear them down and replace them with God's thoughts. Yes, God wants us to connect with other people, but the loneliness will never be defeated until we connect first with our Creator God and recognize how valuable we are to Him!

▍Finish What You Start

Have you ever noticed how many things we start in life but never actually finish? Most people make New Year's resolutions every year and although we usually start off strong and determined, our resolution list quickly thins out until we end up not finishing any of them.

How many of us have started jobs, marriages, hobbies, or exercise and weight loss programs only to quit before crossing the finish line? All of us can look at the history of our lives and see things we never finished in spite of the best intentions in the world to finish.

Starting is easy but finishing is hard. Let me give you a few reasons why finishing is so difficult and what to do about it. People tell me all the time that "this time" they want to finish what they start......only to find themselves back in the same pattern of failure.

The more things you start and don't finish, the more you begin to feel like a failure in life. But you will experience true success when you get in the habit of finishing. However, here are a few things that can sabotage your ability to finish:

1. Our common enemy (Satan) wants to make you think and feel you are a failure. He does everything he can to discourage you from finishing.

2. When you think something is a good idea but you are not 100%committed in your heart to see it through, you are double minded. How do you know you aren't fully committed to finishing? You are double-minded if, when resistance comes, you can be easily talked out of it. James 1:8 says, "A double minded man is unstable in all his ways."

3. Divided loyalties is another reason you fail to finish what you started. This happens when part of you really wants change but another part also likes what you're doing right now (no matter how wrong it is). Your affections being lined up with your heart is key to finishing what you started.

So as you read this today:

a) **Forgive yourself for past failures,** for not finishing things you told yourself that you would.

b) **Before you start another commitment, determine in your heart** and mind that this is what you really want no matter what happens. It could be weight loss, exercise, re-commitment to your marriage, overcoming an addiction, bettering your career or anything else.

c) **Stay focused everyday** by reminding yourself of the consequences of not finishing and the rewards of finishing. (They are quite substantial.)

d) **Finally, remember to trust God.** He gives you the grace to finish everything in your life that will glorify His name and will bring you closer to the destiny He created you for. Trust in Him daily for the strength and courage to be a finisher.

Conclusion: Finishing needs to be a way of life. You will never be truly successful unless you finish what you started. Some of us have unfinished assignments and when we look back we can see that's where the blessings have stopped.

▌ It's Time to Put Your Foot on It

We have all experienced many things in our life over the years and when we think about these experiences, we realize they are very similar and that they actually repeat a pattern. Not only are they similar, but we also recognize that these events have impacted our life on a very deep level… they have even gained some control over our life.

These past events and circumstances have created boundaries that limit our ability to serve God the way that He's called us to. We may not be happy about it, but as time goes on, many of us have gotten used to the limits and have come to just accept things the way they are.

I call this mindset "living in the land of good enough", but it's time to get out of the land of good enough… and the only way to do that is by putting our foot on it!

What am I talking about? I am talking about taking authority and headship over the areas of our life that have hindered us and limited us from going any further in our walk with God. Ephesians 1:22&23, "And He put all things under His feet, and gave Him to be head over all things to the church, which is His body, the fullness of Him who fills all in all."

Before we can begin that journey, we need to identify the problem. It takes an awakening and stirring of our spirits to want to go come out of the land of good enough, to push past where we are today and to want to assure that our life is making the maximum impact.

I pray that every one of us would recognize that it's time to begin to step on the thing that once stepped on us. It's time to take the dominion and authority that God has given to us. After all, He is the head and we are the body and He has put all things under our feet. I repeat....It's time to begin to walk on those things that one time walked on us! Luke 10:19, "Behold, I give you the authority to trample on serpents and scorpions, and over all the power of the enemy, and nothing shall by any means hurt you."

In the book of Joshua, in chapter 10 we read that Joshua sealed the cave where five enemy Kings were hiding. He then brought the kings out and instructed his captains to put their foot on their necks and take dominion over them. Joshua 10:24, "So it was, when they brought out those kings to Joshua, that Joshua called for all the men of Israel, and said to the captains of the men of war who went with him, "Come near, put your feet on the necks of these kings." And they drew near and put their feet on their necks."

This event is symbolic of God bringing the things that once controlled us to the forefront of our hearts and minds. He wants to show us that He's delivering the enemies of our soul before us so we can have headship and take authority over them.

I say that it's time for the body of Christ to put our foot on these things and that we walk in victory. It's time to go further in our walk with God than we have in the past.

But it starts first with an awakening of our spirit. Number two: Having the understanding of the authority and headship that God has given us. Number three: We must remember that Jesus already defeated the enemy. All we are doing is "re-presenting" Jesus and defeating our enemy in the power of His might.

I encourage everyone reading this to put your foot on it! Don't back down…..go forward!

Changing Directions

▌ Go East—Not West!

Someone once said that the quickest way to see a sunset is to go east, not west—referring to our tendency to run away from problems and the darkness in our life. We either bury them or deny their existence.

But, east leads into the darkness because the sun sets in the west and rises in the east. In other words, facing problems will quicken our healing and full recovery. On the other hand, burying or denying problems will prolong the agony, causing more hurt and pain.

Remember the old saying....pay now and play later or play now and pay later. We can't avoid pain because we live in such a dysfunctional, emotionally wounded and sinful world, but we can minimize suffering by running east, not west.

We all want God's resurrection power to deliver us from tormenting thoughts and hurts, but few understand and are willing to take the journey to get there. The bible says there's no resurrection without death and burial, showing us that there's an order and process to our healing.

Go east young man… not west! Face those years of pain and completely close the door on the devil, so he can't use those memories to mess up your life, relationships and destiny.

God's word tells us that weeping may endure for a season, but joy comes in the morning. The joy of the Lord (supernaturally strengthening our spirit) comes out of the darkness we go through. Healing, deliverance, and relief from suffering are the result of confronting our darkness instead of denying, burying and running from it.

We've been running from God without realizing it because we box Him in through traditions and erroneous religious teachings. We've made Him a puppet on a string we think we can pull and make Him do what we want and how we want it!

Yes, God allows us to go into darkness to experience His resurrection power…His unconditional love leading us to face past and present problems. He won't help us run away from them but we can miss Him if we don't understand this great love.

Notice I said, God "allowed"…. not, "caused." There's a big difference between them. Death & burial always comes before the resurrection power of Jesus can bring healing and deliverance in our lives.

Moses lived 40 years in the desert before he became the most humble man, eligible to now be God's deliverer for the children of Israel. David had years of working with the Philistines before God could use him as His vessel. God allowed Job's darkness to show him what needed to change on the inside. Even Jesus went through a dark night of the soul in the Garden to prepare Him to be Savior of the world!

So, when past hurts from what you did or what others did to you show up again, realize that God wants to set you free from them. That's why they're showing up again, but this time don't run west…..face the darkness of your life and run to it!

Going Back... To Go Forward

All of us, in some way or another are still influenced by our past. What I mean by "our past" is how we were raised. Today our lives are still impacted by our parents' weaknesses and strengths; the culture we were raised in; our past memories; the belief systems we were taught, etc. Of course, some of those influences were positive and will remain so in the future. On the other hand, others were destructive and have already sabotaged relationships, finances, lifestyles and especially our walk with God!

Understanding this fundamental truth equips us to begin breaking out of the boundaries set by these past influences, because these things keep us from experiencing the kind of success God created us for.

The bible has a lot to say about these things. It teaches us in Exodus 34:7 that the iniquities of our fathers are carried down from generation to generation, even up to the fourth generation. Have you ever said, "I never want to be like my father or mother" because of their destructive habit patterns? But, have you wound up doing or saying the same things? Do you realize you probably think, cook, keep house, work, act, believe and relate to others the same way your parents did?

Two things stand out to me from my childhood that show me the need to go back... in order for me to go forward.

1. Because my father, his father and his 3 brothers operated a 24-hour, 7 days a week family business, our family life was completely enmeshed with our work life. Everything in our lives was intertwined with the operation of that business. Holidays, birthdays, and everyday life was incorporated with work. There was no separation. I learned early in life that family and work were one and the same.

I became a workaholic and that didn't change, even after I was born-again. I desired to keep every family member involved in the work of the ministry because it seemed natural that family life and work life were tied together. It was implanted in me as a child, along with many other faulty beliefs. It became my DNA, affecting me after I accepted Jesus as Lord.

2. My mother was a great woman, but she had one serious flaw. She was an absolute perfectionist, and that instilled in me a performance-oriented mentality. She controlled me by showing me great love when I performed in ways that pleased her and by withholding love when I didn't. She thought she was helping me.

Because of this I became not only a workaholic, but one who worked hard for approval and acceptance. I was a performance-oriented, driven person! You can imagine the trouble that caused in every area of my life, including my family and my marriage.

The truth is, when I gave my life to Jesus I still lived under the same influences and with the same problems as I had before I became a Believer. Unfortunately, I was taught early in my Christian walk that if I wanted to move forward I should never look back.

Well, all of us have similar stories (if we're honest). We need to break that religious tradition by having the courage to look back and honestly examine our family and cultural upbringing. Our emotional healing and future success as children of God depend on it.

We have to go back before we move forward. Here's how:

1. Get out of denial and break the religious myth that after we're saved, we don't have to deal with our past. 2 Corinthians 5:17 is talking about our spirit, not our soul.

2. Don't deny your feelings. Listen to them because they reveal where and who you are on the inside.

3. Break ties to your family culture Remember, you're in God's family now, so adopt His culture. Jesus told us if we don't love Him more than our mothers and fathers, we aren't one of His.

4. Crucify by repenting and deny things from the past access to your life again, as the Holy Spirit reveals them to you.

5. Finally, embrace your new family's culture and beliefs.

YOU CAN'T GO FORWARD UNTIL YOU FIRST GO BACK!

▍ Set Right Priorities

sn't it amazing how a 20 dollar bill looks so big when you take it to church....but so small when you bring it to the mall to go shopping? Or, think about how long an hour serving God seems to us and yet how minimal 60 minutes seems if it's spent watching TV, playing sports, sleeping, or taking a lunch break.

And, consider how laborious it is to read a chapter in the bible, but we find it so easy to sit down and read 100-300 pages of that bestselling novel. When we're on that big Saturday night date, we have no problem staying up late, but we'll sure complain about losing sleep if we have to get up for a Sunday morning service. Isn't it strange that we're so quick to trust directions from a total stranger if we are lost, believe the advice from the latest pop-psychologist, but we're so hesitant to seek God's direction in the Bible for the issues of our life?

It comes down to recognizing what our priorities actually are. Many of us live our life convinced that loving and serving God is our priority, but in reality we are self-deceived! When examined more closely, our actions will betray us and reveal our true priorities. What should we do about it? Here are a few suggestions.

1. First, repent that you have been living a hypocritical Christian life! Recognize your condition. Admit that, like the Church of Laodicea in the Book of Revelation, your heart for the things of God is lukewarm at best and isn't pleasing to God. According to scripture, the life of a lukewarm Christian is worse than a life without Jesus Christ. At least an unsaved person, when faced with the truth of their ungodly lifestyle recognizes they need Jesus. But, a Christian living an ungodly, lukewarm life style is deceived into thinking that everything is good. The truth though, is that it's not!

2. Next, study His Word to find out what He expects of us who have His Spirit living in us. John 15:1-7 tells us that if we're connected with Him there must be evidence (fruitfulness) of His life in us. We should be obedient to His Word, have a giving nature, show unconditional love for one another, desire to worship and praise Him continually, develop a prayer life and last but not least have a desire to come together as His body on a regular basis to worship Him.

3. Be baptized and filled daily with the Holy Spirit. He is the presence of God and He will keep you passionately in love with Jesus. When the fire goes out, we're all subject to living a compromised Christian life, but the Holy Spirit is available every moment of our life. Get into the daily habit of being filled with His presence. It's as simple as just asking Him to fill you!

4. Finally, I believe it is absolutely necessary to share your faith with someone daily. Too many of us are closet Christians… afraid of rocking the boat. Or we're deceived into believing that we should keep our faith to ourselves. The river of God's love must flow out of us by sharing our faith with others. This allows God to pour more of Himself in us and keeps us in His fresh anointing. Let's rip the veils of deception off our eyes and start living the true Christian life. Let's not buy the lie many Christians are being told today. They believe they're going to heaven but they also don't think there is a hell!

Let's get our priorities straight and start living a truly true Christ-like life. It's worth the effort.

▌ Seeing the Bigger Picture

When life gets hard, the easiest thing in the world is to just quit and give up on our dream. We quit because we aren't looking past our noses. We're too focused on the journey (dream) instead of keeping our eyes on our actual destination. We lose sight of the bigger picture, the reason for which we were created.

Of course the journey to our destination is very important. We can't get to where we need to be without it. But we have to keep in mind that the journey is but a tool that prepares us to be successful when we reach our destination. We can't reach our destination without it.

Unfortunately, too many people get off track along the way. They make the journey their destination, get their eyes off the prize, quit along the way and then never fulfill their life's purpose.

"Are we there yet?" That's the question we always asked as kids on a long car ride. As long as our destination was in sight, we could tolerate the long journey, with its monotony and discomfort.

Keeping the bigger picture in mind (the end goal, the destination) keeps us focused during the journey to that destination. If our dream isn't clearly defined or we aren't fully determined to see it come to pass, quitting our journey can easily become a viable option.

Over a hundred banks turned down Walt Disney when he tried to fund the development of DisneyLand. He was even fired from his newspaper job for lacking ideas, and went bankrupt several times. But he never lost focus of the bigger picture.

How about Thomas Edison? When he was 4 years old his teacher sent a note home saying, "Please remove Thomas from this school because he is too stupid to learn." That opinion didn't keep him from going on to invent the incandescent light bulb, becoming the world's most prolific inventor in history, or having 1,093 U.S. patents as well as many in the UK, France and Germany.

Then there's Lou Ferrigno. As a child Lou developed an ear infection, which resulted in a hearing loss in one of his ears. His father was very critical of him because of his hearing loss, believing he would never achieve success. Yet, at the age of 20 he became the youngest body builder to win the Mr. Universe title and then became a legend on the TV show, The Incredible Hulk. He once said, "If I hadn't lost my hearing, I wouldn't be where I am now." It forced him to stay focused on the bigger picture (his desire to be successful) and maximize his potential.

There are many others who stayed focused on the end game in spite of obstacles they faced along the journey. For example, early teachers considered Einstein an un-teachable fool and Wayne Gretzky (the most famous hockey player to play the game) was told he was too small, too slow and would never make it in the NHL. Believe it or not, they told Beethoven that he was a hopeless composer.

None of these men let the difficulties of their journey deter them from reaching their destination of greatness, because they saw the bigger picture. They accepted that life isn't fair, doesn't give you what you deserve, but it gives you what you demand.

All these men had two things in common: They never quit when it seemed like it was their only option; and they always stayed focused on the bigger picture, their destination—not just the journey to get there.

As we enter into a New Year, let's not allow the old year's journey (no matter how difficult and long it's been) to deter us from pursuing our God-given dreams and goals. There is a prize ahead, so let's press on toward our goal. Like the Apostle Paul said in Philippians 3:13&14, "Brethren, I do not count myself to have apprehended; but one thing I do, forgetting those things which are behind and reaching forward to those things which are ahead, I press toward the goal for the prize of the upward call of God in Christ Jesus."

Handling Crisis

▍ How to Get Out of a Pit

A pit is a dangerous place to stay in for a long period of time, because a pit will kill your dreams, ruin your ministries and even steal your destiny.

In Genesis 37:18-22 &29, Joseph, who seemed to have everything going for him, found himself in a pit. He had God's favor in his life, he operated in great spiritual gifts (dreams) and, as the youngest and favorite son, he was the object of his father's special love.

Joseph's brother Reuben put him in the pit, but his brother Judah took him out. One moment he was in the pit and suddenly he was out of it! And by the way, Joseph wasn't the only one who found himself in a pit. David, Jeremiah, Jonah, Paul and Silas also found themselves in one too.

Pits are a part of life, but staying in them for a prolonged time is destiny-threatening. We can find ourselves in a pit because of personal failure, overwhelming stress in our lives or because other people have put us there. The good news is that we don't have to stay there!

God is about to turn around someone's prison into a garden. If you will follow these steps, your suddenly will happen. What was Joseph's secret for success that can help us get out of our pit?

He kept bitterness out of his heart, which was revealed years later when he met up with his brothers. He told them that what they meant for evil, God meant for good.

He recognized the sovereignty of God and trusted Him for the outcome of his pit experience. He expected God to turn it around. Throughout the bible God reveals Himself as the God of the turn-around. No matter how deep your pit is, recognize God is there with you. He will never leave you nor forsake you.

Joseph never blamed God for the pit. Neither did David, Jeremiah, Jonah, Paul or Silas, so don't blame God or anyone else for your pit experience. If you have, repent immediately and receive God's forgiveness.

Last but not least, Joseph's life praised and honored God. Remember I said Reuben put Joseph in the pit, but Judah got him out. Judah means praise and that's the common denominator with everyone who got out of their pit! They praised and honored God when it wasn't popular or easy to do. It was God-centered, not a self-centered praise. Praise Him with all your heart and you will be setting yourself up for a sudden breakthrough…. You will get out of the pit!

CONCLUSION: God never intended that we stay in a pit because He knows it can become a tomb. Pits are opportunities for new beginnings but what you do with your pit experience is your choice.

■ Overcoming Your Setbacks

A favorite saying of mine is, "Don't let your setback cause you to step back". As I wrote in a previous blog on this same issue, from time to time everyone experiences setbacks. My definition of a setback is, "when the strategies and plans that you made to see your goals, dreams and visions come to pass fail miserably". That is a major setback!

But here is a news flash….. just because your plan and strategy failed, it doesn't mean your dreams and visions have failed. Too many Christians give up when initially their plans and strategies fail. Instead of changing their strategy, they change their dreams. Setbacks are not a signal to quit and give up on your dreams. James 4:7 says, "Therefore submit to God. (His plans, dreams and visions) Resist the devil and he will flee from you."

In this morning's news I read that NASA's space program suffered a major setback. In a preparatory exercise, a million dollar spacecraft exploded before it was even launched into outer space! Their comment was, "We make room for failure." Their vision of launching this spacecraft wasn't changed, even though their initial strategy failed.

Here are some pointers to overcome the temptation to step back from your dreams and to help you stay hopeful.

Be clear about your dreams and visions: Many people aren't convinced in their heart that this is what they really want in their life. It must become a burning passion inside you. My football coach always told our team, "If you want to have a winning season, you must eat, drink and sleep football!" It has to become the all-consuming passion of your life.

Know it's what God wants for your life: It might appear to be a great idea, but.... make sure it's a God idea. God's dreams and visions will stick and are not easily blown away by life's storms.

Make room for setbacks. Proverbs 24:16 says, "For a righteous man may fall seven times and rise again, But the wicked shall fall by calamity." It's okay if you fall down... just don't stay there!!

God's purposes for your life will be tried and tested: Of course Satan will always challenge your destiny, but your flesh can also get in the way and it must be denied. You have to live a disciplined life for God's dreams and visions to come to pass, so count the cost before you go forward. God doesn't always change your challenges, but He will often change YOU to meet those challenges. That's what it means to live by faith.

Trust in God. Ultimately, only He can navigate you safely through all the land mines of life and bring you into your destiny. Trust His word, not what your circumstances or what other people are telling you. Proverbs 3:5&6 says, "Trust in the LORD with all your heart, And lean not on your own understanding; In all your ways acknowledge Him, And He shall direct your paths."

CONCLUSION: Things aren't always what they appear to be. Don't make quick judgments based on your circumstances, allowing the devil to convince you to step back.

▌ Turning Your Crisis into a Turning Point

Most Americans today live a life governed by cycles of personal crises—a phenomena I call "living in crisis mode." The definition of crisis is *a problem, situation, or condition, that's beyond your control or your ability to change.*

Crisis comes in all shapes and forms. One crisis could be receiving a discouraging doctor's report. Another could be your spouse telling you he or she doesn't love you anymore because they found someone else. It could be losing your life's investment, losing your home to foreclosure or a loved one passing away.

These challenges and others like them bring us into crisis mode. The problem is that we can get used to living that way. We become conditioned to accept boundaries created by these on-going crises. When we are in crisis mode, survival becomes our only goal—not complete deliverance, freedom and victory. Or, for those of us with a victim mentality, we can even enjoy living this way, because in a sick way, it gives us much-needed attention and affirmation.

How can our crisis become a turning point? Let's formulate some principles and look at how the woman with the issue of blood (found in Mark 5:25-34) turned her crisis around.

Become sick and tired of being sick and tired: After spending twelve years and all of her money on doctors, she finally got to that point. For some of us, it has taken even longer, and many still aren't there yet. They are still trying to manage their crises. It's like going to "pain management" clinics for the rest of your life instead of finally getting rid of all the pain. You have to get to the point of being sick and tired of being sick and tired. Are you there yet?

Believe the good news: Remember what it says in Romans 10:17, "So then faith comes by hearing, and hearing by the word of God." This woman heard about all that Jesus had done. You can't let God turn your crisis around without having faith in His word. Study the word and take notes on the sermons you hear at church. Bury God's word in your heart, so you'll believe and will also have faith, (two different things). Faith involves: action- acting out God's word and communication- declaring what you heard over your circumstance. As she crawled behind him to touch His garment, she said in verse 28, "If only I may touch His clothes, I shall be made well."

Make the right choice: She chose to no longer manage her crisis, to abandon her own efforts completely and to cry out to God! Your life today is the sum total of all your choices. Today you can make the right choice.

Express your desperation: Desperate people won't let public opinion keep them away from their miracle. In the bible we read that blind Bartimaeus cried out to the Lord with a loud voice, Jairus the ruler of the synagogue forced himself on Jesus in the midst of a large crowd and of course we just looked at the bold actions of the woman with the issue of blood. These desperate people did everything to get Jesus' attention and He responded to them in a positive way.

Although Jesus was in the midst of the multitude, only blind Bartimaeus, the woman with issue of blood and Jairus received a turn-around, so God's presence alone isn't enough. How you express your desperation is individual and personal. There is no formula to it, but it must be done! Are you tired yet of living in crisis?

If you are, you too can turn your crisis into a turn-around. God is waiting for you, so don't just wait for him.

CONCLUSION: The good news is that your crisis can be your turning point. You can make a major change for the better. The devil is more afraid of the dream (seed) you're carrying than he is of you. He wants you to live in crisis mode. So make up your mind today. Say, "This is my day for a turning point!

▌ Your Trials Can Benefit You (part 1)

I t's true that life is full of trials, but it's also true that we often fail to recognize the benefits they provide for us. You're probably saying, "You've got to be kidding!" No, I'm not kidding! Let's examine just a few hidden benefits they provide for us, because to discover these hidden treasures in trials, we must look deeper than just on the surface.

When you're traveling in unknown territories you need a map and a compass. Trials can provide a compass, letting us know if we are on or off course in our journey with God. For example, Jonah was running away from God's will. He lost his bearings, as many of us do at times. Like Jonah, we don't do what we should, and we wander in the wrong direction. God sent a storm to Jonah, and a whale to swallow him and you may wonder where the benefit was in this trial?

Jonah's trial was not sent to kill him. God's grace in action through this trial helped him fulfill God's purpose for his life, saved him from throwing away his God-given destiny and it put him in the right direction. Jonah got back on course and God used him to save a nation from destruction. Could the trial you face today have the same purpose? Are you running from God, knowing His call but wanting to do something else? Is God trying to get your attention to turn you back to His purposes for your life?

In Chapters 4 & 5 in the Gospel of Mark, when Jesus and his disciples were going by boat to the Gadarenes (which means the prize is at the end), a severe storm threatened their ability to reach their destination and even endangered their lives. This trial revealed two important things. When Jesus leads you, the devil himself will challenge you and do everything he can to change your direction.

Trials can be the enemy's stumbling blocks to influence you to change your direction. Check it out by asking, "Is Jesus in my boat, or am I going it alone?" If Jesus is in your boat, the devil is confirming you're on track by the trial you're facing. Be assured, you're close to fulfilling God's plan for you in this season and that this trial will not last very long. They made it to their destination and a demonized man, as well as a whole region, was freed from Satan's control. Their trial couldn't compare to the great victories accomplished by staying on their God-given course.

A setback doesn't mean you should step back! If you endure the trial Satan sent your way, you'll see the fruit of your efforts. Don't give in or give up.

Your Trials Can Benefit You (part 2)

As we discussed in part one, there are hidden treasures of blessings in every trial we go through. But, because we miss the blessings, we fail to celebrate their positive effects. We don't dig deep enough, focusing only on the negative things on the surface. In part 2, let's continue to uncover more benefits and discover how to tap into this gold mine of blessings.

Trials bring us closer to God. Jonah 2:1&7 says, "Then Jonah prayed to the LORD his God from the fish's belly…'When my soul fainted within me, I remembered the LORD; And my prayer went up to You, Into Your holy temple.'" What a change of attitude from this prophet who had been running from God! But it was Jonah's trial that drew him back to God!

Like Jonah, we easily forget how much we need God in every step of our life, until we're in the midst of a great trial. Trials show us how much we've been living as our own god. A good sign we're our own god is that our prayer life is almost nonexistent and our thoughts are centered on "me", not on our need for God.

Trials can bring us to our knees, draw us closer to God and can deepen our roots of faith …..all good things! We also need to remember that trials and storms don't last forever. Their life span is often determined by how long it takes to develop our faith to believe that God will get us out. Jesus said to Peter in Luke 22:31, 32, "And the Lord said, "Simon, Simon! Indeed, Satan has asked for you, that he may sift you as wheat. "But I have prayed for you, that your faith should not fail; and when you have returned to Me, strengthen your brethren." When our shipwrecked faith becomes strong faith, the mountains are removed and we can strengthen those around us.

Trials build character. It's amazing that a piece of coal, under extreme pressure for a period of time, changes from an ugly black object into a beautiful precious diamond! Trials produce godly character by revealing what's in our heart. Pride, selfishness and rebellion are hidden inside until the storms squeeze them out! Jonah's trial gave him the right perception of himself. From the belly of the whale he said in Jonah 2:8&9, "Those who regard worthless idols Forsake their own Mercy. But I will sacrifice to You With the voice of thanksgiving; I will pay what I have vowed. Salvation is of the LORD." His character was changing and he was reflecting the true and living God. Does your character reflect Him?

Trials develop patience as we read in James 1:2&3, "My brethren, count it all joy when you fall into various trials, knowing that the testing of your faith produces patience." Each storm we go through has the potential of developing patience, in other words... endurance. I'm not referring to the endurance to accept whatever Satan brings through those storms. I'm talking about enduring confidence, trust and faith in God's ability to deliver us out of every trial!

The heat of the fiery furnace won't make us back down, step back or give in because we will endure to the end. We believe what it says in Matthew 24:13,"But he who endures to the end shall be saved." And what it says in Philippians 1:6, "being confident of this very thing, that He who has begun a good work in you will complete it until the day of Jesus Christ."

Whatever you're going through, you're going to come out of it. The question is what will you come out of it with? Instead of letting trials go to waste, get all the God-given benefits you can from them. At the end of his trials Joseph told his brothers in Genesis 50:20a," But as for you, you meant evil against me; but God meant it for good...."

Having the right attitude in the trials of life will help us discover God's blessings and benefits.

Gaining Financial Wisdom

▌ Getting Out of Debt (part 1)

The way the economy is going, life is getting increasingly difficult and the financial forecast doesn't look very promising either. It's obvious that things are about to get worse, but, how
does God weigh in on all of this? Does He care about finances and
does He offer any practical solutions to the problem of debt? Well
first of all, Jesus spoke more about money than any other subject in
the bible. I know that's shocking, but it's true.

I believe Jesus highlighted the money issue because He knows
that debt and poverty are manifestations of the kingdom of Satan.
They are curses that are often carried down from generation to
generation. Through money, the enemy attempts to control and
hinder our lifestyles and ultimately our destiny. It's amazing how
many of us are scrambling every day just to get enough money to
live on, leaving us very little time for God. How ironic, since God
is the true source of our lives! Matthew 6:33 says, "But seek first the
kingdom of God and His righteousness, and all these things shall be
added to you."

Let's look at a few God-inspired principles to help alleviate debt
and poverty in our lives. They are not in any particular order, but
they point the way to apprehend God's plan and strategy for us.

Believe He is a debt-canceling God: MARK 11:24,"Therefore
I say to you, whatever things you ask when you pray, believe that
you receive them, and you will have them." He cancelled all of our

debts on His cross two thousand years ago. In other words, believe that God wants to deliver you from poverty and cancel your debt. Nothing happens unless we believe.

All poverty and debt originates from sin: Any time you or your ancestors trusted in money and wealth to meet needs instead of God....that's sin. 1 Timothy 6:10, "For the love of money is a root of all kinds of evil, for which some have strayed from the faith in their greediness, and pierced themselves through with many sorrows." Identify with the source of that sin, repent in the place of your ancestors and then repent for personal participation of that sin in your own life. Debt and poverty must be cut off at the root in order to break that cycle in your life. These two steps of identification and repentance are foundational to getting out of debt. For further explanation of this, please go to our website www.stophurtingstarthealing.com and contact our office.

Review your spending habits: Is God in the decision-making when it comes to your spending habits? Many of us don't allow God to be Lord over this area and we spend according to the lust of our flesh, not the leading of the Holy Spirit. If we examined our spending habits every day, we'd learn some shocking truths about our own heart. List all of your spending for seven days, bring them before the Lord in prayer and ask Him if there needs to be any changes. If you're sincere, you will probably see that radical change is necessary. That's a good time to ask God's forgiveness for your idolatry (putting money ahead of God).

CONCLUSION: These steps reveal your true desire to have poverty and debt broken over your life. A lot of us talk a good talk but when it comes down to it, that's all it is....talk. Getting out of debt requires a radical change in our view of money and our understanding of God's desire to be God (the only source) in and over our lives. We will continue this series tomorrow.

▌ Getting Out of Debt (part 2)

Yesterday I gave three foundational steps to get out of debt and break poverty over your life. Here they are in review, but for more details read yesterday's blog.

Believe that God is a debt canceling God.

All poverty and debt is rooted in sin.

Review your spending habits.

Today I will start with step #4, which is tithing.

Tithing is the key to having God's provision released in our life. This godly principle is the one that Satan opposes the most in a Christian's life. It pertains to the "law of the first fruits" which simply says that the first part of any fruit you produce belongs to God. Tithing is part of that law. The first fruit of our income (10%) belongs to God and the 90% that is left is ours.

In the book of Malachi, God promises that if we don't rob Him and we give what rightfully belongs to Him, He will release His abundance, provisions and protection. Always remember: God's ways are not our ways. If we expect God's word to fit our logic and understanding, we'll miss Him every time. It comes down to these two questions about our tithes: Is Jesus really Lord over our life? Do we really want to get out of debt?

Break the curse. Poverty and debt are curses that won't go away unless forcefully broken. Matthew 12:11 says, "And from the days of John the Baptist until now the kingdom of heaven suffers violence, and the violent take it by force." In other words, Satan and his demons must be forcibly removed from our life in the name of Jesus. We can assume that we are under the effects of a curse if we experience a cycle of negative events repeating over and over again. We break free, only to fall back into the debt cycle again. Sometimes expenses rise out of nowhere, our car breaks down, we lose a job, etc. If they happen consistently, it is a sign that a curse of debt and poverty is over our life.

Here is how to break it according to God's word.

Identify that it's a curse. Galatians 3:13&14 tells us Jesus became a curse for us so that we could have the blessings of Abraham (including prosperity). Declare, "In Jesus' name I break the curse of poverty, lack and debt over my life!" If you haven't done step two from yesterday's message, add it in this prayer and declaration.

Release the blessing of prosperity, abundance and multiplication in the name of Jesus. This is a war that must be fought in the spiritual realm and the weapons of warfare are not carnal….they are spiritual.

Constantly renew your mind with God's word. Remind yourself that you live in God's kingdom, not Satan's anymore. Your God is generous and desires that you live the abundant life Jesus purchased for you. He made provision for you to be prosperous for His kingdom purposes (if you are doing His works, not your own). Ask yourself, "Why do I want to get out of debt and have poverty broken off my life?" If your answer doesn't include something like being Jesus Christ's representative; you've missed the whole purpose of your redemption!

CONCLUSION: By applying all six steps to your everyday life; deliverance from poverty and living in debt is a sure thing. The greatest challenge is to recognize that Satan doesn't want you to be financially free because then he can't control your life. This is war and you must be in it to win it! Stay in the fight and don't give up..... BECAUSE OF JESUS WE WIN!

Finding Purpose & Fulfillment

Receiving Your Tomorrow Today

Do you believe that God has many more blessings that He still wants to pour out in your life…that you haven't yet received all He has for you? Well He does. I call them "blessings on God's lay-away plan", because God has them on hold until you're ready to receive them. But the good news is that you can have these future blessings now.

We need to stop putting limits on how and when God will bless us. We limit Him by believing the lie that we can only get certain blessings in this present season. We think we have to live out that season before we receive the future blessings God has in store for a different season. In Genesis 26:1-13, Isaac is in a season of famine—not just a drought where you can plant and get a limited harvest. No, in this famine there has been no rain for years and the ground is so parched that nothing grows. It certainly isn't a season to plant, yet God tells Isaac to do just that.

You can imagine that everyone watching Isaac plant his garden thought this foolish man had lost his mind! But when all was said and done, while everyone lived by the natural laws of the earth, Isaac was obedient to God and lived by the supernatural laws that govern the kingdom of heaven. As a result, he received a great blessing out of season. Isaac received tomorrow's blessing today.

Let's stop being narrow minded. If you make excuses why you can't receive God's "layaway" blessings out of season, allow Satan to set boundaries on God. Maybe you're suffering a famine in your finances, your marriage or your emotions, going through a season of depression. You can get God's blessings (healing, deliverance, breakthrough) right now, no matter what season you find yourself in. God is eternal and He's not subject to time or natural laws. He will even violate natural laws to release the stored up blessings He has for your life.

Follow these steps to begin to see your tomorrow today:

1. Know that all of God's blessings have been freely given to you. (Ephesians1:3) They are yours to have in this season. God's name reflects that He is always a "now God". He told Moses, "I am that I am", not, "I was or will be". Jesus purchased your blessings when He died on that cross for your sins 2,000 years ago. He made you eligible and qualified to receive all of God's promises right now.

2. Stop blaming the season you're in for the lack of fruit in your life. As long as you live in the circumstances of the past, you will never walk into your destiny. Remember, your feet won't take you where your mind won't go.

3. Partner with God by mixing His promises with faith by sowing God's seeds (words) in the season you're in (Hebrews 4:1&2). In other words, believe God's promises are meant for you today, even if you're in the worst season of your life. "How do I sow seed?" you ask? God's promises must be rooted in your heart (imagination). When you can see it in your imagination, start speaking God's promises everywhere you go. (If you can see it, you can have it!)

4. Expect ridicule and opposition from other Christians who don't believe God's word. Ignore them! That's Satan's way to discourage you. But be encouraged. God's blessings are always contested by the enemy.

Why wait for tomorrow's blessings when you can have them today? Your believing will cause you to receive it.

How to Handle the Unexpected

t seems like almost every day we face an unexpected event. Of course some events are more serious than others, but these unexpected happenings either make or break our day. But, if we think about it, many unexpected things could have been avoided if we took God's spiritual law of sowing and reaping seriously. Galatians 6:7 says, "Do not be deceived, God is not mocked; for whatever a man sows, that he will also reap." What you sow today determines what you reap tomorrow.

In Matthew 13:24-30 there is a parable about tares and wheat. While the farmer slept, an enemy sowed tares in the midst of the wheat, so at harvest time he was shocked to see tares, but the parable is meant to show that because he fell asleep and didn't pay attention; the tares were able to be sown.

Although this parable is in the context of an agricultural society, it's also true for us. We're "sleeping" if we don't watch the seeds (words) we sow. Proverbs 18:20 says words produce fruit, "A man's stomach shall be satisfied from the fruit of his mouth; from the produce of his lips he shall be filled." So the bad harvest (words-tares) is expected, not unexpected.

Your life right now is the sum total of all your words about yourself and your destiny. Take inventory of the words you release into the atmosphere. Words from your heart and out of your mouth release life or death over your destiny, as it says in Proverbs 18:21,

"Death and life are in the power of the tongue, and those who love it will eat its fruit."

Seemingly unexpected events really aren't, and can be avoided in the future by disciplining your tongue. Release today what you want to see happening in the future, because what you sow today, you'll reap tomorrow.

Now.... what about the truly unexpected events in your life that you aren't responsible for? Here are a few points to consider when dealing with them:

GOD IS SOVEREIGN: Not every problem will be removed, but can be used for your good. God's desire isn't to kill you or let Satan kill you. He's in the character-building business; building the character of Christ in you. Trust His sovereignty because He loves you and ultimately controls your destiny. ROMANS 8:28," And we know that all things work together for good to those who love God, to those who are the called according to His purpose. "

KNOW WHEN TO RESIST: If what you're going through is outside of the will (word) of God; if it's contrary to His purposes for your life and has Satan's fingerprints all over it..... you MUST resist! If you're not sure and fear you'll miss God, trust the Holy Spirit to show you for sure in the Word. James 4:7, "Therefore submit to God. Resist the devil and he will flee from you. "

TRUST IN GOD: In the parable of the wheat and tares, the tares were allowed to grow until harvest season, when they would be separated from the wheat. Some unexpected things can't be changed, like a lost loved–one or if something important is taken away from you. In those cases we can only trust in God and let Him use it for our good. Proverbs 3:5, "Trust in the LORD with all your heart, and lean not on your own understanding;"

THANK GOD IN ALL THINGS: 1 Thessalonians 5:18b, "in everything give thanks". Notice it says to thank God IN everything, not FOR everything. GOD is there with you even in the unexpected, and if God is with you.... no weapon formed against you will prosper!

Conclusion: Unexpected things will always occur; they're part of life itself. But, they don't have to stop God's destiny from being fulfilled, if we handle the unexpected correctly.

▌ The Key to a Fulfilled Life

L ocked up on the inside of every person, there is untold potential to lead a successful and fulfilled life. The sad story is that most people will never see that potential realized because of this truth… found in just three words…..lack of discipline!

Yes, I believe discipline is the key ingredient in our life that will unlock the greatness that God created in us. What is the simple definition of discipline? It can be summed up in just two words….. delayed gratification! This is the concept of paying now- playing later instead of playing now- paying later.

Discipline means planning long term success by sacrificing instant and short term rewards, because short term rewards eventually lead to long term failure. Most people want discipline, but never achieve it and as a result they're living unfulfilled lives.

There are no short cuts to being disciplined, but these suggestions will help you on your way to a fulfilled life:

1. Schedule the pain. In other words, practice "advanced decision-making". Determine what areas in your life need the most discipline and decide what you're going to do about it. Literally, develop an action plan; that's "advanced decision-making". Don't wait until the last minute every day to make the necessary changes that unlock your great potential. For example, if you decide your physical condition is the most urgent area in need of discipline, don't wait every morning to decide whether you're going to exercise and eat right that day. Your mind will convince you you're too tired to exercise and it's okay to skip one or two days. But, if it's in your calendar, the decision's already made and you will do it. "Advanced decision-making" helps you to schedule your pain.

2. Practice your discipline: Are your motives for being disciplined right? Do they glorify God and advance His kingdom, or are they selfish reasons?

Pre-plan; don't wait for the last minute. Set at least a six-month strategy in place before you start.

Remember, Satan will resist you in your thoughts, because that's where the spiritual war is fought. Discipline starts in your mind first before it can overflow into your actions. Proverbs 23:7a says, "For as he thinks in his heart, so is he.." Reading and memorizing God's word helps you to stay focused in your disciplines. Remember that delayed gratification doesn't mean there's no gratification. The best is yet to come and will eventually keep coming.

Be consistent. Many people start, but never finish, so make up your mind to see this discipline through to the end.

You don't have to do it alone. Make yourself accountable to others. God created us to be accountable in our relationships so we can support one another in things like discipline. Ask 2-3 people to hold you accountable. Most importantly, depend on the Holy Spirit to help you. He is your Comforter and will give you the encouragement and strength to be disciplined, unlocking the great potential in our life.

The ability to live a fulfilled life is knocking at your door, no matter how young or old you may be. Choose the area that needs the most discipline today and start by taking that first step. By reading this you have already taken your first step!

Making Your Daily Life Better

I f you could change three things in your life today to make it better what would they be? For many of us, it's a few little things and not big things that make our day bad or good.

One way to discern what those two or three things are is to recognize what your life priorities really are. The following question will help you identify those priorities.... What would you want to accomplish if you knew you only had one year to live?

The truth of the matter is that not one of us knows how long we have to live here on earth. Hebrews 9:27 says, " And as it is appointed for men to die once, but after this the judgment," so in reality we should live everyday as though it's our last. Now, go ahead and make a list of what you would like to accomplish before you go home to be with the Lord.

By the way, it says in John 14:6, "Jesus said to him, "I am the way, the truth, and the life. No one comes to the Father except through Me." So if you're planning on spending eternity with God you better make sure Jesus is your Lord and Savior. Remember, religion can't save you... only Jesus can.

When you make that list you'll notice that even if it isn't long you still haven't gotten to your top priority to make each day better. There is another important step and it's broken down as follows:

1. Arrange your list of priorities if you had only one year to live in the order that is most important to you.

2. Next, compare the first priority with the rest of your list. For instance, let's say this is your order of importance: family, relationship with God, financial security, health, weight, etc.

Since family in this example was #1 priority, compare it to the rest of the list and put a check mark on the one you think is more important. As family is compared to finances, I realize that family is more important so I put a check by family. Next, I compare family with health and realize that without good health my family life would be affected. Although family was originally my priority, I put a check by health too. Continue with each one from the top to the bottom of the list and the one with the most checks actually becomes your main priority.

Now if you add that one priority every day... your day would instantly become better. If you added more than one, imagine how fast you would improve your every day? Awareness and discipline is all it takes.

As Christians we have an advantage and that is the power of the Holy Spirit! But if you aren't filled with the Holy Spirit yet; you can be. If you have accepted Jesus as your Lord and Savior, just ask your heavenly Father as Luke 11:13 says. "If you then, being evil, know how to give good gifts to your children, how much more will your heavenly Father give the Holy Spirit to those who ask Him!"

Start having better days. The choice is yours!

▮ What Matters Most

People don't care how much you know... until they know how much you care! I believe that these words of wisdom are so true.

We often hear people's frustration because the important people in their life don't listen or receive instruction from them. It can be parents with their children, teachers and their students, or sometimes it's the boss and his employees. Whatever the situation; the bottom line is that people won't take our advice if they don't feel genuinely loved or cared for by us.

If we think about it, how do WE ourselves often react when others correct or teach us? We walk away feeling like they were trying to show us how much smarter they are. Or we sense that they're looking down on us, judging or controlling us and trying to make us feel that they're the better person. If that is our perception, we won't believe they truly care and we won't listen to them.

Now, in all fairness, many times that's just not the case. The other person may really care and want to help us, but because of the disconnection between us, it seems like they don't really care about us or our circumstances. We end up shutting out their words from the very beginning of their conversation.

Since people are only interested in what we know if they believe we genuinely care about them, here are some things to show them that you care:

82

1. Start your conversation with a question about their life and circumstance instead of immediately giving them all your wisdom and advice. Find out what's on their heart and what they are going through. Be a good listener before unloading the wealth of your opinion! We must earn the right to speak into a person's life before we can be effective.

2. Don't just listen; be a good listener. Make eye contact, responding with caring facial expressions and concerned looks, because your body language reflects your care and concern for their well-being. In fact, many times your body language speaks louder than your words and if they contradict each other, the other person will immediately pick up on that.

3. Avoid distractions and interruptions such as texting, phone calls, doodling, etc. during your communication time. These things send a wrong message and will literally cause the person to shut down to whatever you have to say before you even say it.

Prepare to avoid these distractions ahead of time by turning your phone off and putting it out of sight. Let everyone know you're unavailable during your time with that person. Avoid sitting next to a window that looks on a busy area, so you and the other person can stay focused on your discussion.

4. Put aside enough time so they won't feel rushed, or they'll immediately shut down to what you have to say. It takes time to be a good listener and also be able to express your thoughts. However, there should be a time limit, so be truthful and up front about how much time you have available. You can always agree to another meeting with them to show that you really care and are willing to see their issue through to its conclusion.

It takes time, energy and commitment to genuinely care for someone else, whether it's a child, a spouse or a friend. Remember, what matters most is that we really care about one another. And ..... this matters most to God! Ephesians 4:32a, "And be ye kind one to another, tenderhearted,...."

Making Good Life Choices

▌ Discerning the Right Decision

So many of us are at a crossroad in our life; not knowing what decisions to make. We're struggling with choices like; should I marry him or not; where should I invest my life savings or should I invest at all; should I move or stay where I am; do I retire now and risk not having enough or do I continue working; will a divorce end this pain or do I stick it out and hope for change; etc. Making the right decision is crucial, but the wrong decisions on critical issues can set our life back many years and even cause us to miss our God-given destiny.

The gift of discernment is one of the greatest (and most-often overlooked and under-used) gifts from God. Every human has natural discernment, based on their accumulation of experience and knowledge, to help make right decisions. Unfortunately, natural discernment is "hit and miss and" and often fails.

God has never and will never fail! That's why I'm talking about supernatural discernment, His wisdom, given through the Holy Spirit, to make the right decision in any situation. The right decision fulfills His destiny for us; a destiny of joy, peace and prosperity (not failure, depression or hopelessness).

The question of the day is… how do I get God's discernment… how does it work?

Simply ask for the Holy Spirit (Luke 11:13). He is the source of every spiritual (supernatural) gift. Remember, it's a gift. It's not earned as a reward because we've been a good Christian for years. It's for anyone who accepted Jesus as their Lord and Savior and who is Spirit-filled. If this doesn't describe you; take the time to make that decision. It has nothing to do with your successes or failures; God desires to bless you just as you are. But, you have to make the choice to receive this great gift that will literally save your life!

Here is how it works. The Holy Spirit gives insight into the choices confronting you. For instance, in choosing to divorce or not, the Holy Spirit supernaturally reveals God's mind concerning that potentially devastating decision. He also reveals who is influencing you to make that decision. If a friend or family member is speaking into your heart, the Holy Spirit reveals what is influencing them. Three sources influence decisions… a human source; a demonic source or a God source. If we can't detect what is influencing us, we can easily make the wrong decision, end up devastating our life and hindering our God-given destiny.

Too often we've forged ahead with bad decisions, regret them today and are suffering their consequences. Don't live with just natural discernment when you can have God's gift of discernment! Matthew 7:7, " Ask, and it will be given to you; seek, and you will find; knock, and it will be opened to you."

The Holy Spirit is available to you so……Don't dare make another decision without God's help!

God Left the Giants in the Land

D id you ever wonder why our all-powerful and awesome God left giants in the Promised Land for the Children of Israel to contend with? And why did He also leave them for us to face and to struggle with?

He's God and He's in control, so He could have easily removed them from our life. But I want to suggest to you that He left them for the following reasons:

He allowed them to remain in our life so we recognize our need for Him. Every struggle we have points to our weaknesses and our need for God's help.

Giants in our lives help us discover God's strength and His willingness to help us. We get to know ourselves better. Things get revealed in us that we would have never discovered if everything was going well.

Giants are in our life so we can learn how to fight the good fight of faith. Life will always challenge us with troubles and struggles. We must be prepared to develop the spiritual muscles to face stronger giants that will surely challenge us in the future.

There is no victory without a battle. We experience God's great victories only when we defeat our Goliaths.

Finally, the size of the reward we get in victory is in direct proportion to the size of the enemy we defeated! Many of us are about to truly get blessed because the giant we are facing today is huge.

CONCLUSION: The next time we face our giant we need to give God thanks as He says in I Thessalonians 5:18, "in everything give thanks for this is the will of God in Christ Jesus for you." We need to remember that God is doing something awesome in our life. Instead of trying to avoid the struggle, we should embrace it because it's working for our benefit.

Know that although the battle is ours to fight, God is with us in every swing of the sword (word). Romans 8:31 "What then shall we say to these things? If God is for us, who can be against us?"

▍ Life is Hard, But God is Good

This past week I've been in the Book of Ruth, preparing for the Women's Bible Study in September.

The book opens at the lowest point in Ruth and Naomi's lives. Both women are wrapped in a blanket of grief.

Life doesn't always turn out the way we think it should, does it? Death of a loved one, divorce, infertility, financial loss, sickness.... Things that we didn't plan on, invade our lives.

What do you do when you're paralyzed with grief? How do you handle it? These are questions I asked myself not long ago when I was in a season of grief.

Working through grief is no easy task. It's a process that doesn't happen overnight. Everyone grieves differently, but everyone must grieve in order to heal.

Because grieving impacts us spiritually, emotionally and physically, all three areas need to be considered:

Spiritually

Keep praying. Have honest conversations with God about what you're thinking and feeling. Lean on Him for comfort and reassurance.

Have someone pray for you who knows how to pray for inner healing.

Resolve any unfinished business. Ask God's forgiveness for any failures on your part. Extend forgiveness for any failures on the part of others.

Stay in God's word daily, it's a healing balm.

Emotionally

Surround yourself with a strong support system. Having people around that love and care for you is essential. Don't isolate yourself.

Give yourself permission to cry. Expressing your emotions honestly and openly as often as you need is vital to the grieving process.

Release your resentment if you have any unresolved anger regarding your loss. Take the time to list your resentments along with the causes. Then release each offender and hurt into God's hands.

Physically

Get sufficient rest. Grieving will often affect our sleep. Getting proper rest is important to both your body and emotions.

Get a balanced diet. Eat healthy, don't skip meals. Stay away from junk foods and caffeine. Drink plenty of water.

Get daily exercise and sunshine. Both cause your brain to release endorphins that will release a sense of well-being.

Each of our lives is like a story, one we have been writing since birth. Some chapters are good, others not so good. It's important to remember that your story is not finished yet. If you are breathing and alive, there are always new pages to write.

You will recall, Naomi and Ruth were stuck in a storyline of grief, pain and loss…. No hope for their future.

Little did they know they were about to embark on a new chapter. The same God that Naomi believed had "made her life very sad," was about to move in ways she never dreamed possible!

If you're in a season of grieving, don't give up. God's imprint is on the pages of your life. He has amazing things in store for you. God is good....there is always victory at the end.

▌ Making the Right Decisions

Everything we do begins with a decision and every day we make a multitude of them. Each decision brings with it good or bad consequences; consequences that will be compounded daily. It's time to stop blaming everyone around us for where we are today and recognize that it's because of our own decisions!

Our destiny is determined by the decisions we will make today and although we can't do anything about our yesterdays, we can still influence our todays and tomorrows. The God of all creation has planned a great life with a great ending for us, but our decisions can hinder those plans.

In Deuteronomy 30:19-20, God reveals the incredible power and privilege of choice we have been given and He encourages us to make the right choices. But, He also warns us of the serious consequences of making wrong choices.

The responsibility of having God's awesome plans and purposes fulfilled in our life is squarely placed on our shoulders and no one else's. Here are some obstacles affecting our decision-making process that should be avoided.

People's opinions probably influence our decision-making more than anything else. We make decisions (consciously or subconsciously) trying to please people, looking for their approval and acceptance. We can avoid this by knowing how valuable and special we are in God's sight. Stop trying to be a cheap copy of a great original! When God made you, He threw away the mold. If He wanted you to be somebody else, He would have made you somebody else. Low self-esteem and a poor self-image directly influence our decision making, so spend time with God and allow Him to reveal your true identity.

Faulty motives such as seeking attention, personal approval, self-gain, ego, and pride also influence our decisions. We need to ask God to search our hearts for the reasons behind our decisions. Galatians 6:8 says, "For he who sows to his flesh will of the flesh reap corruption, but he who sows to the Spirit will of the Spirit reap everlasting life." We should use our God-given freedom to make decisions that will advance His kingdom not our own.

Ask yourself these following questions:

Will the decision I'm about to make promote God and His agenda or me and my agenda?

Will God receive all the glory from the decision I'm about to make?

Will this decision focus the attention on God or me?

Money issues affect a lot of our decisions. We can be blinded by the power of money and controlled by the lust of our flesh that money appeases. Mark 6:24b says "You cannot serve God and mammon." Money can be a huge factor in deciding who we hang out with or who we won't; who we serve and who we won't serve; who we will go out of our way for and who we won't. We become a "respecter of persons" based on how people can benefit us.

Many other factors affect our decision making; things such as ethnic, family and religious traditions, prejudice and faulty beliefs can influence us more than we realize. We need to remember that making right decisions is not just simply saying yes or no; there is a lot behind every one of those choices.

Since this issue is so critical to our destiny, wouldn't it be a good idea to take our time before jumping into a decision? Let's think it through and invite God into the process so He can reveal what's really influencing us and help us discern if it's God decision or just a good decision!

Our life's destiny depends on right decisions, so let's make a quality decision today about our decision-making process.

Movement Doesn't Always Mean Progress

We often confuse the business of "doing" things in life with "making progress" in life. The children of Israel come to mind as a good example of this, wandering about in the desert for forty years, but never reaching their destination. According to experts, their trip from Egypt to the Promised Land could have been accomplished in 11 days. They certainly had a lot of movement... but very little progress! Here are some examples of how we confuse movement with true change and personal growth.

Christian Maturity: People are convinced that because they do things for the Lord, they are spiritually mature. They say things like, "I go to church three times a week, I'm part of the choir and in my spare time I even pray for the sick." Those are all good things to do, but spiritual growth is best measured by whether or not we act like the Lord; if we are Christ-like. The fruit of the Spirit we exhibit is the tool to measure true godliness. In describing this deception, 2 Timothy 3:5&7 says, " Having a form of godliness, but denying the power thereof: from such turn away. Ever learning, and never able to come to the knowledge of the truth." Paul tells Timothy that "religion" doesn't assure someone has godliness, or they understand the power of God or that they are mature Christians.

We talk it but don't walk it: We're deceived if we believe we've changed by the movement of our mouths, not our feet, because talking change doesn't mean that we ARE changed! I previously wrote a blog titled; Change Is Not Change Until It's Changed.

Some people are convinced they've turned the corner because they talk as though they've changed. In reality they are like the children of Israel; just going around in circles. You see this in marriages; a promise to change is made, but you never see any progress in their relationship with each other. We also see this pattern (movement without progress) in dead beat employees, or substance abusers promising to change. In the parable in Matthew 21:28-31, Jesus compares two sons. One didn't fulfill the promise he made to the father. The other one wasn't willing at first, but changed his mind and actually did the work his father asked him. Jesus said that assuredly, the one who did the work was the one who did his father's will.

What are we to do? It is frustrating when we realize we haven't made any progress. But, here are a few things to help us come out of the deception that motion alone means progress.

Clarify your goals: Too often we have double vision concerning the destination of our life's journey. We'll never hit a target if we have double vision. James 1: 7&8 tells us a double-minded man is unstable in all his ways and won't receive anything from God.

Don't take short cuts: We all like the path of least resistance, but the easy way and the shortest way is often the wrong way. People offer us ways to get rich quick, a simple way to make our marriage work, lose weight without changing our eating habits, etc. But they never work!

Don't try to save your life: It's impossible to avoid making the personal sacrifices necessary for true progress to take place in our lives. We must carry our cross daily and deny our fleshly desires to walk the road of progress. The faster we accept the truth that progress requires sacrifice, the faster we will make true progress. There's no progress without a cross.

Conclusion: Let's stop wandering around our mountains, substituting movement for progress. It is Satan's great deception, so let's wake up and stop comparing ourselves to the world's measure of progress. But instead, let's measure our progress according to God's word.

▮ Take Off the Mask

When we go through painful events in our lives, we have a tendency to want to sweep our feelings under the rug and ignore them, hoping they go away. However, by failing to deal with our hurts and losses, we create a perfect environment for depression and despair to overtake us.

When we mask these hurts and losses to protect our hearts from things we don't want to face, it wounds our spirit and affects every aspect of our lives. Our spirit, soul, thoughts, feelings and emotions, our physical health and well-being and even our relationships are impacted. Masking our feelings will block our spiritual growth, stunts our emotional and mental maturity and eventually hinders our intimacy with God and others.

We need to take the masks off and let God begin the healing process. Don't ever fear admitting the reality of your pain to God. He'll work in and through your suffering to reveal His plans. He will protect you from wrong decisions, keep you connected with people who He pre-destined to be part of your life's history and will separate you from those who aren't.

If you are transparent before God and allow Him to have access to your heart; He can give you wisdom and understanding about your destiny in Christ. David told God in Psalm 51:6 "Behold, You desire truth in the inward parts, And in the hidden part You will make me to know wisdom."

These following four steps will help remove your masks. They will set you free from the darkness surrounding you so you can enter into God's joy, peace and happiness. I call these the "five D's":

Determine: What sad experiences or significant losses and hurts from the past haven't you faced? They can be things such as: divorce or death of parents, rejection, failures, false accusations, unjust criticism, thwarted goals or unrealized dreams. These may be with you from childhood, buried deeply in your unconscious minds. But, just because you don't think about them now, it doesn't mean they're not affecting you today (because they are).

Discover: Find the source of your masked pain through earnest prayer such as, "Oh father, I come to you as a child seeking Your help. Let Your peace calm my troubled heart. Please make me aware of my need for healing and show me Your truths in my inward thoughts and feelings. Bring to my mind hidden hurts I have masked and the circumstances that caused them."

Define: Each event had an emotional impact on you. Define them with specific statements such as: "_____ made me feel _____"... "I am grieving over_____"... "I was so embarrassed when _____"... "I felt abandoned by_____"... "I was really hurt when_____"... "I determined to never let _____happen again."

Pinpoint and define the hurts and losses you've masked all this time. Let God take you out of denial and into inner healing. You may have been weighed down for years, but make this your year to escape the heaviness you've been living with for so long.

Decide: Deeply and genuinely grieve your hurts and losses. Release forgiveness to those who have hurt you and receive God's forgiveness for holding anger or hatred. There is no justification for anyone with the nature of Jesus Christ to harbor these things. You may also need to forgive yourself for wrong choices that have perpetuated the pain. Ecclesiastes 3:1&7 says, "To everything there is a season, A time for every purpose under heaven:….. A time to tear, And a time to sew; A time to keep silence, And a time to speak;"

Deepen: Take your dependence on God to a deeper level, trusting that He can give you emotional freedom. Allow the Holy Spirit to pray through you daily. He's your physician, your medicine cabinet and He has every antidote you need to make you whole. The Lord desires that you be whole in your spirit, soul, body, and relationships.

May this holiday season be depression-free! May the clouds of hopelessness and despair be lifted off you. May God's wonderful plans for your life be revealed to you. Remember, He supplied you with everything you need to accomplish them. But first….. TAKE THE MASK OFF!

▌ The Tipping Point

I t doesn't take a lightning-quick mind to recognize that the world is in turmoil and in great trouble. We've never been this way before. Look at our own nation for a minute. Not long ago we led the world in higher education (we now rank 27th), technology, economic stability and high moral standards—to just name a few. Do you know what we now lead the world in? Hint: it's not any of the things I just named.

We now lead the world in the highest national debt; meaning the money we borrowed and have to pay interest on. Our debt is over 16 trillion dollars and it's increasing by 6.6 billion dollars daily! We lead the world in the most prisons, capital crime, abortions and the most gay and lesbian population. This is not a list to be proud of!

We're in trouble, on the verge of no return and I believe we're at the point known as "the tipping point".... when you go too far one way and can't go back. I know I'm not the only one who has heard the sound of the alarm, the warning from God concerning this season. Joel 2:1 says, "Blow the trumpet in Zion, And sound an alarm in My holy mountain! Let all the inhabitants of the land tremble; For the day of the LORD is coming, For it is at hand" So what should we do about it? Well, here is what I heard in my spirit. See if it agrees with yours.

It's time to return to our first Love. Without God there's no hope; but with Him all things are possible! Let's admit that religion can't change anything and it has only made things worse. Only God's tangible presence can save us from this tipping point. *Return to God* simply means praying for a greater hunger and thirst for Him. It means repenting for trusting in man's ways rather than in God and His word. It means to stop playing church and turning away from religion (dead works) and rituals that block true intimacy with God. It means humbling ourselves by having one agenda: the desire to know, to experience and to please Him. He reveals Himself to people who are desperate for His tangible presence. God says many times in His word, "If you return to Me, I will return to you."

As the body of Christ, we must hear the urgent sound of the alarm, put differences aside and come together, wherever… however, to pray. God's people need to wake up to the power of corporate prayer. (There are many different ways to accomplish that).

Rampant individualism in the body of Christ today blinds us to our need for one another. Just because others are sleeping doesn't mean you should stay asleep too. As an individual you can make a difference by not staying silent. Make noise, sound the alarm, shake the leaders of your local church. We don't have time to be politically correct anymore. This is the real thing, and we're at a tipping point; so we must shake off of our drunken stupor and be the "kingdom leaven" God called us to be.

The only difference between the true church and the rest of the world is His presence being manifested in and through us. Moses told God that he wanted to enter the Promised Land only if His presence went with him. Moses knew that the only thing separating the children of Israel from all the other people is God's presence.

Let's wake up and recognize we're at a tipping point in our personal lives, in our local church, in our nation and in the world! We can make a difference and prevent the rapidly approaching disaster. There is no turning back, so let's return to the Lord!

▌ What Is Your Life Plan?

There is a famous and very truthful saying that goes like this, "those who fail to plan, plan to fail". Most of us know we need to plan for our careers, vacations, jobs etc. but for whatever reason; we very rarely make a LIFE PLAN.

The bible says in Proverbs 29:18a, "Where there is no vision, the people perish (amount to nothing)". In other words, if there is no vision (plan) in a person's life, they will not fulfill their God-given destiny. This is especially true for their personal life.

So, what's a LIFE PLAN? Well, a LIFE PLAN is made up three components: goals, strategy, and accountability. Let's begin to make a LIFE PLAN for ourselves by asking ourselves a few questions.

1. GOALS: What are my priorities for the next few years? Make a list (in no particular order) of the four or five things you consider most important to accomplish in your life. Compare them to one another and number them in order of priority.

2. STRATEGY: What do I need to add to each day of my week that will help me to accomplish my priorities? (GOALS)

Add just one thing (the same one) each day until it has become a daily core habit. After you are doing it at least 5 out of the 7 days for one month, add one more item until four new things have been incorporated into your daily core habits.

Example: if my priority (GOAL) is to lose weight, on a daily basis I would determine to restrict my caloric intake. After this has become a habit I would then add walking daily as my exercise.

3. ACCOUNTABILITY: As part of my daily strategy, who can I connect with to hold me accountable in keeping my goals?

One reason our New Year's resolutions usually start failing after a week is that we don't follow up our goals with a strategy and accountability.

Choose someone with similar priorities and who is serious about making a LIFE PLAN for themselves. Don't choose people who will go easy on you or themselves. Pray about your choice and ask for God's discernment.

Conclusion: Many of God's people are living far below the level of success that God intended them to have because they don't have a LIFE PLAN. They wander in circles, repeating the same mistakes over and over again.

Why don't you take the time this week and deeply think about your God- given destiny? Make a LIFE PLAN following the guidelines you just read. There are also a lot of good books on this subject of life planning. We plan for dying.... LET'S PLAN FOR LIVING FOR JESUS!

Managing Your Attitude

▮ Change is a Choice

We can't arrive at a place of productivity and destiny in our lives without making adjustments (change) along the way. We've heard so often that the very definition of insanity is believing you can keep doing the same thing you have been doing over and over again and yet expect to get different results!

I guess that puts most of us in the insane category, because we do just that. Even if they don't work, we repeat the same patterns of behavior in our marriages, relationships, job, finances, or our personal and even spiritual growth. Then we wonder why we aren't successful. The truth is: We will never reach true success unless we embrace a lifestyle of change.

Change is here to stay, so we need to just accept that we'll never reach a point where we're no longer confronted with it. Many of you would reply, "But I've already changed." Well, I have to tell you. Change is not a once in a life time event. It has to be embraced as a way of life.

We're all on a "journey to significance" in Jesus. The truth of the matter is that God's forever leading us into opportunities to change so we'll fulfill the destiny He created us for. In fact, what you're going through right now is all about your need to change. It's giving you the perfect opportunity to see the areas God wants you to change.

I've said many times....change is not change until you change! Sure, we talk a lot about change, the need for it and the promise to do it, but in reality we never really do it. That's because we're too busy defending the "status quo". We say things like, "That's how I've always done it!" or "I just want to hang on to what I have left!" or "I'm okay, I can make this work!"

People are in love with the image of success but they aren't interested in the process of success. Success always includes change, so we have to break free from our old wineskins if we want God to give us His new wine. New revelation of who God is won't fit into our old habit patterns.

Our core habits have to change and I believe that by changing just one core habit for one month we can radically change our life. Change will lead to more change...it creates a chain reaction.

Here are some basics to living a life of change:

1. Change must be tied to God's purpose and vision for your life. Discover His destiny for you so you won't just be a cheap copy of a great original!

2. Learn to color outside the lines. Many of us are so used to conforming that we shut down our God-given creativity. Dream again and think outside the box. Get out of that stinking rut you've been conformed to fit in over the years.

3. Don't be afraid of the unknown. Remember, the unknown isn't the impossible. Be willing to launch out into the deep at the bidding of God's word. He's attracted to your faith, not your feelings and unfortunately your feelings resist the unknown.

4. Change isn't ever possible without taking a risk. When David confronted Goliath there was a definite possibility he would die. When Abraham left his land to follow the Lord, he took a tremendous risk.

Sure there's a risk factor in every opportunity to change, but if we always avoid taking risks, we'll end up living a mediocre life, always trying to maintain the status quo. Constantly avoiding fear of failure, rejection, making a mistake etc. keeps us away from our destiny.

You're on a journey to significance, so don't miss your opportunity to be a champion and world changer for Jesus by resisting change. Remember.... CHANGE IS A CHOICE! Make the right one!

▌ Don't Let Your Setback Cause You to Step Back

believe somebody today needs to hear this from God, because you're just about to give up on a dream, vision or a promise that God gave you awhile back.

When it comes to our God-given dreams and visions, from time to time we all suffer setbacks. But we have to remember that everything we do for God will be contested, challenged and resisted by the devil. Too many of us get discouraged and give up when we hear from God, begin to walk it out, but then face immediate frustration and failure. Sure, it's a setback, but it's no reason for us to step back and give up on our God-inspired dream or promise. Here are some steps to prevent failure when you are pursuing God's promises in your life.

1. You have an enemy: but it's really not Satan directly ....it's you. It's the weaknesses of your own flesh (feelings and emotions). We need the discipline to be influenced by God's word rather than our circumstances. 2 Corinthians 4:18 says, "While we do not look at the things which are seen, but at the things which are not seen. For the things which are seen are temporary, but the things which are not seen are eternal. "It takes daily discipline to die to our own ways, thoughts, and feelings and stay focused on God's promises.

2. A setback doesn't mean that the dream or vision was a lie. If your strategy fails it doesn't mean that you're a failure or the dream or vision isn't from God. Just change your strategy. The promises stay the same, but the strategies can change.

3. Timing is everything to fulfill God's plans and purposes in your life. Live on God's time clock not your own. Many people step back when it's not happening according to their time plan, forgetting that God said "my thoughts are not your thoughts and my ways are not your ways". Just wait on the Lord and trust that He knows what He's doing. His promises will always come to pass. "My promises are yea and amen." Don't quit on God..... He hasn't quit on His Word that is in you.

4. Let God purify your motives. Ask, "Why do I want this vision, dream or promise fulfilled in my life?" We can suffer setbacks because our hearts are still too filled with selfish motives. The advancement of God's Kingdom should be our ultimate goal. I agree that we should prosper and enjoy divine favor not just for ourselves but for those we can influence in the present and future. God will put His dreams, visions and promises for us in a holding pattern because we have the wrong motives.

5. Forgive yourself if you stepped back. God hasn't changed His mind concerning His promises in your life. Don't let discouragement turn into depression and stay in your life. You always have a choice to once again embrace God's dream, vision or promises.

Conclusion: No one is perfect, but God loves us and desires that we succeed in every way. So don't give up or quit when you have a setback. Remember…setbacks are only permanent when you step back!

▌ Jesus, Lord Over Your Thoughts

I f you are struggling with tormenting thoughts or with thoughts that cause you anxiety about other people or yourself; let me make a suggestion. There is an answer to your problem and that answer is to allow Jesus to be Lord over your thoughts. Having His authority over our thoughts is an awesome, wonderful blessing; a gift that He has given to us.

Usually when we think about Jesus' authority over our life we just think about it being over only our actions and over the choices we make; and that is true. We do need to make Him Lord and have His authority over every aspect of our life, but every action and choice begins with the thoughts we have concerning that issue. It all starts in the thought realm as it says in Proverbs 23:7, "For as he thinks in his heart, so is he."

It is amazing how many people really don't like themselves and they even reject themselves. It's one thing to have the people around you reject you; but it hurts on a much deeper level when you reject yourself. Some of us don't need much encouragement to reject ourselves and let's face it; there is always somebody who doesn't like what you do or what you say or what you look like. It just reinforces what our own thoughts are concerning your own value (even our value to God.)

You may wonder, "How do I actually make Jesus Lord over my thoughts?" That can only be accomplished when we bring our thoughts into alignment with God's word. The bible says in Romans 12:2 that we need to renew our mind daily so we can change the way we think. And Jesus tells us in John 6:63 that His words are "spirit and life."

If we call upon the name of Jesus and ask Him to be Lord over our thoughts, we can tear down the strongholds that make us think badly about ourselves. We will see everything begin to change. You know, having Jesus Lord over our thoughts will affect everything about our life.

Today why don't you make Jesus Lord over your thoughts? In other words, examine your thoughts with the light of God's word and if they don't line up with God's heart, His will and His intention for your life replace them. Find out what God says about your circumstances and begin to dwell on that instead. Reject any thought that doesn't line up with the way God sees you, declare Jesus is Lord and replace it with what God says.

Especially with this holiday season fast approaching us, we will be spending time with some people who pressure us and "squeeze" our emotions! Let's make this year different and not let our joy to be sabotaged. Let's not enter this Christmas holiday with a sense of dread.... and the way to do that is to invite Jesus to be Lord over our thoughts. If we do that, we will find that the very people we have shunned in the past will be the ones that we can now embrace. It will be easy for us to reach out to them and release the love of Jesus that He has deposited in our hearts.

▌ Making Life's Troubles Work for You

No matter who you are, there will be times in your life when troubles arise. When they do come, we have to put our life on hold and feel our comfort zones get shaken. One day as I was complaining to God about the horrible problems I was facing, the Lord spoke to me through 2 Corinthians 4:17. It changed the way I looked at any trouble I had to face.... forever! As I read, " For our light affliction, which is but for a moment, is working for us a far more exceeding and eternal weight of glory," three things immediately jumped out at me:

1. Every trouble we face is temporary. Compared to what Jesus went through and the tragedies that many others face, our troubles really are light. Of course, to us our troubles never seem light while we are going through them. But one thing we all must admit; every trouble is not forever. The good news was that any trouble I faced was not going to last the rest of my life! THIS TOO SHALL PASS.

2. God's word also told me that my troubles would work for me. They were temporary AND they would turn out for my benefit. To tell you the truth, in the midst of it I couldn't see how the trouble I was facing could ever work for my benefit. But, how many of you can now look back and see that although your past troubles were rough, it all worked out for the better?

These are just a few ways that my life's troubles have worked out for me, but I'm sure you could add to the list:

Change of direction: from a direction we didn't know was destructive at the time to a successful direction today. We get a clearer understanding of our God-given destiny.

Confirmation: knowing which values are important and which ones aren't and then committing to live them in our relationships, our God-given time on earth, our ability to influence people for Jesus, etc.

Greater trust: we learn to recognize God's involvement in our lives and trust Him more than ever before.

Thankful heart: we learn to thank God for what we do have rather than complaining about what we don't have. We realize how good life really was before the trouble entered our lives. We wake up to recognize how selfish we were.

3. The last thing God spoke to me through that scripture was that the best was still yet to come. His word says that my light trouble (as compared to what JESUS went through) would work for me a destiny that would release His Glory in and through me and would also increase His favor in my life. I would be a greater influence to others for Jesus.

Conclusion: of course we're never going to pray for God to give us more trouble so we could get all these benefits. But it sure does help us to navigate through today's problems if we recognize that God's hand is on us and our circumstances. We can confess Romans 8:28 with confidence "ALL THINGS WORK TOGETHER for good to them that love the Lord and are the called according to His purpose"

▍ Only One Way

There is only one way we can (and must) live our Christian lives.....it is being Holy Spirit led. We can't please God and be successful in our walk with Him without the Holy Spirit. That's why Jesus told His newly-saved disciples they couldn't be released to share Him with the world, until they were filled with the Holy Spirit. Luke 24:49, "Behold, I send the Promise of My Father upon you; but tarry in the city of Jerusalem until you are endued with power from on high."

Jesus knew that the Holy Spirit dwelling in them would give them the supernatural power to be His witnesses on earth. Acts 1:8, "But you shall receive power when the Holy Spirit has come upon you; and you shall be witnesses to Me in Jerusalem, and in all Judea and Samaria, and to the end of the earth." Without it they were no different than any other religious person in the world. Well, if that was true for His first disciples, then it's still true today for us, His 21st Century disciples.

If you are wondering what a Holy Spirit-filled Christian looks like, here are a few identifying marks:

They are people who are very aware of their need for the Holy Spirit's presence in their everyday Christian life. They seek His council, guidance and empowerment in everything they do.

Holy Spirit-filled people have a personality of humility and meekness because they failed miserably when they tried to live a

120

Christian life in their own wisdom and strength. An atmosphere of deep humility surrounds them because of the brokenness in their lives. They understand it's not by their own might, nor by their own power, but it's by the Holy Spirit!

God's unconditional love flowing through them is very evident. They easily forgive those who offend them and are quick to ask forgiveness when they offend others. You like being around them, because God's river of compassion and mercy flows out of them. Jesus said when the Holy Spirit is in us, rivers of living water will flow out of us. John 7:38, "He who believes in Me, as the Scripture has said, out of his heart will flow rivers of living water."

Since the Holy Spirit is the source of spiritual gifts (God's character), if filled with the Holy Spirit, we can walk in the supernatural. This is evidenced by speaking God's language...tongues. 1 Corinthians 14:2, "For he who speaks in a tongue does not speak to men but to God, for no one understands him; however, in the spirit he speaks mysteries." It's also seen by laying hands on the sick and watching God heal them and by having an impartation of God's discernment, wisdom and knowledge so we can "re-present" Him in our life.

So, to live a successful Christian life, we must be Spirit-filled. The original disciples, filled with the Holy Spirit, turned the world upside down and if it was good enough for them, it's good enough for His present-day disciples. Unfortunately, most of us Christians today are turned upside down instead of us turning the world upside down!

What's missing? It's the Holy Spirit. Make sure you are filled with the Holy Spirit and are living a Holy Spirit-led life. Check for true evidence of His presence. If it's not evident, right now ask the Father to fill you with His presence! He promised to give it to you in Luke 11:9-13....you won't regret it!

Maximizing Your Potential

▌ What's In Your Heart?

According to God, what matters most in a person's life isn't our outward appearance, but the condition of our heart. So I ask.....what's in your heart?

What's really in our heart comes spilling out for all to see every time life puts the squeeze on us and we find ourselves in a crisis. That's when our heart truly gets revealed.

It's easy to do and say the right thing when life is going our way and everything is smooth. But, when life becomes pressurized and chaotic and the squeeze is on, our response tends to paint a more accurate picture of who we really are!

There is an old saying, "what's down in the well comes up in the bucket". On the outside we may all look the same, saying and doing the right things ...... at the right time ... to the right people. But what's really inside? What do our hearts really look like?

Our prayer should be like David's as he cried out to God in Psalm 139:23&24, "Search me, O God, and know my heart; Try me, and know my anxieties; and see if there be any wicked way in me. And lead me in the way everlasting."

Knowing your own heart's condition is critical to fulfilling the destiny God created you for. But, a lot of people are afraid to have God reveal their true heart condition to them.

They're afraid, because to see the truth about their heart would mean they would now have to face the truth about themselves, which could lead to self-condemnation. They are afraid because they might not like themselves and would have to admit that some of the negative things people have been saying just might be true.

Our self-esteem is so fragile, that for many of us, if we're shaken or challenged in any way, we fall into a tailspin of failure and a state of deep depression and hopelessness!

For some of us, getting to know our heart is simply out of the question. Yet, every day, because of God's faithfulness and love, He reveals our hearts to us. Jesus said in Matthew 12:34b, "Out of the abundance of heart the mouth speaks". So, a good way to see what's in our heart is by paying attention to how we speak to one another.

Do we respond to difficult people in anger or with patience and love? Do ugly words of revenge spew out of our mouth to people who have hurt us? Do we respond to sudden changes in our life with unwise decisions and harsh judgments, or do we rest in the promises God gave us?

Knowing your heart is imperative and will help you to:

1. Know your real motives behind what you do and say. It gives you an opportunity to align with God's heart.

2. Recognize the many hurts deep in your life and understand your need for inner healing. It will help you to stop blame shifting and cause you to take responsibility for your own actions.

3. Know your own giftedness and be content and confident in how God made and blessed you to be you, not somebody else.

4. Get out of denial concerning your sins so you can repent, ask and receive forgiveness and truly be set free from Satan's torment in and over your life.

God revealing your heart to you is the best thing that can happen, because then change can take place in your life. His love for you is so awesome that He'll take the time to help you know your heart today and every day. So, don't be surprised if some crisis or pressure soon comes and puts the squeeze on. As your heart goes.........so goes your life! What's in your heart?

▋ What's Right Isn't Always Fair

We often can confuse what is fair, with what's right, but God isn't a God of fairness… He's a God of "rightness". He deals with us according to our needs and I'm sure you agree that we have different needs. Philippians 4:19 says, "And my God shall supply all your need according to His riches in glory by Christ Jesus." If one person needs one hundred dollars to meet their need and another needs a thousand dollars and God blessed them accordingly, it wouldn't appear fair but it would be just (God deals with our needs, not our wants).

In our natural understanding we often accuse God of being unfair and a respecter of persons. I am thankful that God isn't pursuing fairness but that he is pursuing justice…. what is right. When we try to be fair we end up being people-pleasers instead of God-pleasers.

As the crowd watched a prostitute wash Jesus' feet with her hair, He told them she loved much because she had been forgiven much. Because of her life style of excessive sin, her need of forgiveness was greater than most. The Lord was moved with compassion by her need to be forgiven and He forgave all her sins, so she expressed her great gratitude with her great act of love. When you see God's grace and favor poured out on someone else, don't be judgmental and accuse God of not being fair. Be thankful that your need isn't that great. Celebrate God's mercy for them.

Picture the following example. Three men were standing in a row. The first man had a smiling and peaceful face, the second had a look of worry and concern, and the third man was weeping uncontrollably. When Jesus approached them, He smiled at the first man, didn't say a word and walked right by him. He stopped in front of the second man, grabbed his hand and said, "Son, everything is going to be alright". When He got to the third man, He hugged and kissed him on the neck and expressed great compassion and understanding towards him. The question was asked...."Who did God love the most?" Many of us would conclude that He loved the third man because He showed more love to him than the other two. Our next conclusion would be that God wasn't fair to the other two men, especially the one He didn't even touch as He walked by.

But, this is how God looked at that situation. The first man truly trusted God's word and the promises he was given. He knew who his Savior really was and was confident He loved him. When Jesus walked by and smiled, He was confirming His love and pleasure in him. The second man was worried and fearful and Jesus' touch encouraged him to trust Him like the first man. When He finally got to the third, He knew this man hadn't experienced His great love for him like the first man did, so He poured out His great love in ways that would touch his heart. He did was right... but to the natural eye it didn't seem fair.

Conclusion: We sometimes miss what God is doing in our lives because our eyes are on other people. God doesn't deal with us based on our human needs and standards. He sees the beginning, the middle and the end of our lives simultaneously and bases everything He does on the destiny He created us for. Thank God for what He has already done and expect Him to always finish what He started in your life. He is not a respecter of persons. Remember, He is a just God and although many times it doesn't seem fair, be confident that it is right. Don't let human judgment get in the way of His present and future blessings. God is a good God all of the time and all the time He is a good God!

Change Isn't Change Until It's Changed

We all talk about the need for change in our lives: How things will be better when they're changed; and yes, we're sure going to change them…well, maybe not now, but very soon. A lot of us talk about change our whole life without ever really changing at all. The problem is: Talk is cheap. Change is not change until it's changed!

One problem is that we really don't know what to change in our life and how to go about changing it. Also, we don't always understand the real purpose of the need to change. Proverbs 16:7 says, "when a man's ways please the Lord, he makes even his enemies to be at peace with him."

I propose the following 6 questions to help you identify changes that are needed. If you answer honestly, they will assist you to start the process of change.

What do you like about your life today? List things you are already doing in your life that you really like. It may not be very long. It might surprise you, since most of us never took the time to think about it.

What don't you like about your life today? This list might be longer because most of us identified what we don't like a long time ago.

Do you feel trapped by the things you don't like? Not every bad thing is holding you hostage, but there's usually one or two things that make you feel absolutely trapped. You have accepted them as a way of life, so you haven't considered what it would be like if they were gone. Write them down now.

If you had only one year to live, what would you like to accomplish? What one or two things would make you feel you accomplished the purpose of your life? These are what you want to leave as a legacy.

What's keeping you from accomplishing the life you want? Pin point things that hinder you from having a good day and a good life. This list might come down to just one or two things.

You have identified the most important things that must change if you really want to see a change in your life. It may not be what you thought, because now you're viewing things through God's eyes, not the world's or your own eyes. You're finally at the point of meaningful change. Now for the last question:

How do I accomplish real change in these areas? The final victory is in completing this last step.

Follow Proverbs 16:3 "commit your works to the Lord and your thoughts will be established." Ask if this is His will. Is this what He wants you to change? Sometimes we want to change the people around us, but many times God wants to change us instead.

Trust that God will help you. "The steps of a righteous man are ordered by the Lord." True change is God's work in our life, not our own efforts.

Implement the God-inspired changes every day, not just once. We'll slip into old habits if we don't do the new things daily until they're core habits. It takes major awareness and effort.

Finally, accountability is the icing on the cake. Share your decision to change and what the changes are, with those who care about you. Ask them to hold you accountable and give them permission to correct you when you slip back from those changes.

Conclusion: Change isn't easy, but it's necessary to grow and be more Christ-like. Decide to begin the process of change today. Unfortunately many talk about change; complaining about the need to change…but they never will. Don't be one of those people. Remember: Change isn't change until it's changed!

▌ **Discovering Your Destiny**

E very person and every people group has a destiny. God created us with an individual destiny, but as we connect with one
another, we become a "people group" such as a family, business, city, nation and a church. God brings people together who are
like minded. He takes our different parts and the different aspects
of our individual calling and out of it He forms a group destiny. As
we identify our personal destiny, we help to advance the call of the
"people group" known as the local church. This in turn affects our
local community, city, state, nation and even the world. "The sky's
the limit!" (As one brother said) concerning God's ability to work
in and through us.

But, unity is the key. In the days of Babel, God was attracted
by the unity of men with evil hearts, so He came down to see what
they were doing. Genesis 11:6, "And the LORD said, "Indeed the
people are one and they all have one language, and this is what they
begin to do; now nothing that they propose to do will be withheld
from them."

We will never truly be part of a group until we discover what
our individual destiny is. You and I are one small part of the whole
but it's an important part. Like our body, each cell structure is individual and distinct, but must connect with other cell structures to
form a healthy, functioning body. The cells need to work together
with others to frame a bigger picture.

If we don't understand our individual call, we will slow down the process of unity. We need to remember that when we are in unity God can use us to accomplish great and amazing things, even if we are a people group that's small in number. (One chases a thousand and two will put ten thousand to flight!) It will take some good quality time to think about our lives and discern what God's plan is for us. But, it's worth the time to discover His plan and connect to the local church so we can know that we are effective members of the body of Christ.

1.) Look at the things you are very passionate about —not just through human emotions or some pleasurable high. I mean passion to the point that you're willing to lay your life down for it.....that kind of passion! That passion goes deep inside and really makes up who you are. The Holy Spirit will help identify those things, but you need to give it time.

2.) Recognize that you might be passionate about two or three things, so discover the one you are the most passionate about. It doesn't mean God won't use you in the other areas, or that you won't have an effect, but they will all support your one major passion.

3.) Connect with a local church. When you identify your passion, you identify your destiny, but then you will want to connect with a body of Christ that cares for your destiny. The right church will have a direction through its purpose and vision that clearly indicates its future. You will know how you fit, where to join in and how to partake of the local church destiny.

The local church is only as strong as the individual person, but because we are in unity, our power and influence will increase, affecting everything around us. Through the local church, the body of Christ can fulfill God's heart here on the face of the earth. Remember, He is the head.... we are the body.... we have a group destiny, and He's placed all things under our feet! Discover your destiny!

■ Having a Good Ending

We live in a world that's made up of cycles and seasons. This speaks to us about new beginnings and good endings. I say good endings because everything has a beginning and an end, even when it comes to relationships.

If you are in a leadership position, whether as a pastor or a business person, learning how to have good endings is critical if you want to reach the vision and destiny God has for you. If you are like me, then that isn't your strong point and it can also be your Achilles heel. I know it is for me, so I want to list a few reasons why it can be difficult for many of us and discuss what we can do about it.

1. Everything isn't forever: It's important to know that God places people in your life for certain seasons to help you accomplish your destiny. Just like a tree that needs pruning every season, some relationships on your team need to be pruned if you are to succeed in God's call. (John 15:1-3) Letting go can be difficult if you don't discern the difference between loyalty to a person and being faithful to God's call. Not having a good ending will damage a friendship and hinders the progression of God's destiny in both your lives. (By the way, let me make it clear that I'm not talking about marriage or any covenant relationship.)

2. You need to see endings as a normal part of life: Life produces more relationships than are necessary and like a fruit tree, when pruned, some fruit will also be pruned. It's important to know which business or ministry relationships need to be pruned because some of our relationships are meant to be forever. Knowing which ones need to be pruned takes the Holy Spirit's discernment.

3. You need to face reality: Pain always serves a purpose. When relationships drain you or your resources there must be an ending at some point. That involves pain....but with a purpose.

4. Sustainability: Again, if a team member is constantly draining you and your resources, in the long run it will affect your sustainability. There must be some ending somewhere.

★ I recommend you read Dr. Henry Cloud's book, "Necessary Endings", because it really helped me understand why certain things in my life had to come to an end. It also showed me the negative results of not having a timely ending and the importance of having a good ending.

▌How Do You Want to be Remembered?

Every single day, you are writing the story of your life. The chapter you are working on right now is being read daily by the people around you. The full story will be read by many others long after you are gone.

I have good news: You can know how your story is going to end, and you can even write the ending before it happens. How is that possible? Here are some ways you can accomplish that:

1.) Learn to say no to the good, so you can say yes to the best! Each decision you make has short term results, but it also shapes your future. Your today is the result of all the decisions you've made to this point, and your tomorrow is the sum of the decisions you make today. So, never make permanent decisions based on temporary circumstances because you have to manage the fruit of that decision for the rest of your life.

2.) Don't accept the agenda that someone else mapped out for your life. Live your life the way God created you. You never want to be a cheap copy of a great original! Ephesians 2:10 says, "For we are His workmanship, created in Christ Jesus for good works, which God prepared beforehand that we should walk in them." Find out what God created you for by reading His word and listening to the voice of the Holy Spirit. Choose to walk in His ways no matter how much pressure people place on you to conform to their ways. Remember, you're writing your own history.... not theirs.

3.) Every day you must manage your thoughts before you can manage your life. Like decisions, your thought life greatly influences your destiny. Nothing else affects your decisions like right or wrong thoughts, so allow Jesus to be Lord over your every thought. After all, a good idea doesn't always mean it's a God idea. Don't jump to conclusions until you are certain your idea leads to the ending you desire. Avoid negative thinking because once your mind is tattooed with negative thinking, your chance for long term success is diminished.

4.) As you change your thinking, start to immediately change your behavior. Take action and begin to act the part of the person you want to become. The problem is that people want to "feel" instead of taking action, but that never works. The faith walk is not the same as the feeling walk! James 2:20 says, "But do you want to know, O foolish man, that faith without works is dead?" The world says if it feels good, then do it. God's word says whether it feels good or not, just do it.

5.) Stay focused on the end. Don't allow the spirit of offense to distract you and take you off track. So many people have their wheels stuck in the mud of offenses and they aren't advancing to their original goals. Remember, planning your end is a daily thing so consistency is non-negotiable. To be remembered the way God intended you to be depends on the consistency of your daily routine. Success is not a "destination thing".... it's a "daily thing". Don't let Satan take you off track through people offending you.

Remember, what you become tomorrow, you are becoming today. Live everyday of your life wisely. Our time is the greatest resource God has given us and the bible warns us about protecting it in Ephesians 5:15-16,

See then that you walk circumspectly, not as fools but as wise, redeeming the time, because the days are evil.   (Eph.5:15-16)

Plan your tomorrows today and be assured that your ending will be what God (and you) want it to be!

How to be the Best You

You're here to become the best version of you…. not somebody else! Who wants to be a cheap copy of a great original? When God created you, He threw away the mold and nobody in this world is exactly like you.

As it says in Genesis.1:26, you were made "in the likeness and image of God." Likeness refers to your spirit and image refers to your body. All human beings are God's highest order of creation, yet God individually hand crafted each one of us (as Psalm 139 tells us). No one on this earth has your fingerprints or your abilities.

The following are some keys to become "the best you":

1. Identify with Jesus: Too often we identify with the wrong people, comparing ourselves with what our current culture tells us is the most popular and accepted type of person. The fashion world and Hollywood set the standard of what's in and what's out, what we should look like and shouldn't look like. But our identity must be in Jesus, our Creator and role model of what He created us to be. Ephesians 2:10 &5:2 tells us to imitate Jesus and know we have a pre-planned destiny. He set the plumb line for us and we can identify with Him by renewing our mind through His word.

2. Refuse to compare yourself with others: Everyone has a call, with different gifts and talents. Stop making idols of people by copying them and living outside of your call because you can do what others can't.

Don't fall into Satan's trap, becoming a copycat and missing out on your God-given destiny.

3. Celebrate who God made you to be: Thank God for how uniquely He made you. You'll embrace yourself as God's special creation and will value your gifts instead of complaining that you don't have the same gifts as other people have. Celebrate yourself as God's "one of a kind" creation, made to His exact specifications, and you will have greater self-confidence and boldness. You'll fulfill His plans and purposes for your life.

4. Refuse to allow people to compare you with somebody else. People suffer from a poor self-image and low self-esteem because they were compared to others. Growing up I was always compared to other children. My report card and other achievements were always compared to the other children's. I was asked, "Why don't you do things or get grades like so and so?" For many years I had low self-esteem because I compared myself with others and came up short.

Parents do it, mates do it, employers do it and even friends do it, but we can refuse to listen! Politely say, "If God wanted me to be like them, He would have made me to be them. But God wanted me to be me, so He made me." Be bold about your personhood. That doesn't mean you can't improve, but improvement is about being a better you, not a better somebody else.

Practice these few keys every day, value your life and people will start valuing you as well. To change the way people see you, change the way you see yourself.

▌ How to Have More Good Days

very one of us could testify that we have both good days and bad days and unfortunately most would say they have more bad ones than good ones. What determines whether our days are good or bad is what I call "core habits".

Core habits can be good or they can be very destructive. Although we have both in our lives, they often go unidentified. We just go through our day without paying too much attention to our core daily habits because we are too consumed with regretting yesterday and how we can change our tomorrow. We forget that in order to change the big picture (our destiny) we have to first change the small picture (today).

We all have good days and bad days, but ask yourself this question. "What makes good days good and what makes bad days bad? Make a list of both on a piece of paper. Remember that the bible says in Psalm 37:23, "The steps of a good man are ordered by the LORD, And He delights in his way." By taking one step at a time we are getting closer and closer to the fulfillment of our destiny.

Here are some things that would make a good day for me. Let me share them with you:

- Getting seven hours of sleep

- Spending one hour of prayer, meditation and reading God's word

- Eating a healthy diet

- Drinking one gallon of water

- Exercising for one hour

It's so important to write down the things that help you have a good day. They become your daily strategy and will radically change your destiny. Now, if you look at your list and see that you are far from accomplishing it on a regular basis, add just one new core habit to your day instead of three or four.

I would say that if you implemented that one core habit 80% of the time for a month, you could consider yourself to be successful. You can then add another core habit, repeating the process until you have implemented all the core habits that make for a good day!

This strategy will help you to have good days most of the time, rather than just having a hit and miss experience. By reviewing your daily core habits and replacing the bad ones with just three or four good ones one at a time, you could change your whole life around. Isn't it worth the effort?

Again, if you just take the time today to review what makes a good day, you will begin the process of increasing the good days in your life and you also will be reaching your destiny. Remember, Satan your enemy, wants you to be consumed with the urgent... not the important. Stop having bad days and start having good ones! It's all in your power.

Life Doesn't Give You What You Deserve

At one time or another, we have all said, "life isn't fair!" Every one of us, over the course of our life has been dealt a bad hand. When this happens we wonder, "What in the world did I do to deserve this?" After searching our hearts and our actions to make some sense out of our circumstances, we finally come to the conclusion..... "Life ain't fair".

Although that's not necessarily a wrong conclusion, it shouldn't disqualify us from the abundance of great blessings that God has promised us. I used to think that what God said in His word and what we could actually receive were two different things. In other words, the bible was just a good story but not something real in my life. I accepted the unfairness of life, believing that the fulfillment of God's promises wouldn't happen until I went to heaven!

Well, that is so far from the truth. Yes, life doesn't give you what you deserve, and it's true that life is unfair, but life WILL give you what you demand. What do I mean? Let me explain. Since God created everything by His spoken word, (and Jesus IS the Word) everything in creation must submit to the Lordship of its Creator. God said, "Let there be"....and there was!

His way of doing things hasn't changed and never will, because He will never change. That's not my opinion. That's what God says. Malachi 3:6a, "For I am the LORD, I do not change. Hebrews 13:8, "Jesus Christ is the same yesterday, today, and forever." Isaiah

144 Maximizing Your Potential

40:8, "The grass withers, the flower fades, But the word of our God stands forever."

When we own God's promises and demand life to bow to the living word of God, it must yield to its Creator and to His word. Let me further explain though, that there are conditions to His promises, but unfortunately some of us are too lazy and would rather complain about how unfair life is. This victim mentality conveniently excuses us from being accountable and responsible for our own life. It's easier to just blame others.

But, if you refuse to be a victim and you want to see the bible come alive in your life, here are some keys:

1. Take ownership of God's promises. He wasn't teasing you when He said He would supply all of your needs according to His riches in glory. He loves it when you hold Him to His word because it proves you believe Him.

2. Don't give up if you don't see results right away. Too many believers stop short of the manifestation of those promises because they lack patience. "God's promises are always yea and amen" and they will come to pass because God is not a liar. His word will prosper wherever He sends it!

3. Go to war. The resistance to the promise isn't coming from God. It's from Satan. So, aggressively submit to God (His word) and resist the devil, confident that he'll back down. Satan's testing to see if you really believe God's promises. He has no power to resist God's word when you declare it from your heart. Praise Him in the night because joy comes in the morning.

4. Don't lose your passion for God's promises. We may start out with zeal, but as time goes on it's easy to get distracted and lose our focus and passion. Jesus said in Matthew 24:13, "But he who endures to the end shall be saved." This isn't only about us. It's also about the people within our sphere of influence. Stay "otherly" and selfless in your walk with God so your victories and blessings can overflow to others. Keep the fire burning in your heart by being a true worshipper of God.

Remember, life doesn't give you what you deserve but it will give you what you demand. Stir up your faith and boldly demand God's promises to be manifested in your life. Start living the abundant life that God has freely given to you..... but was purchased by the precious price of His Son's life!

It's Never Too Late

Sometimes we give up believing God for things, but I want you to know God hasn't given up on wanting to bless you with them. He wants us to believe Him in our relationships such as friendships, marriages and divine appointments. He wants us to never let go of our dreams, financial goals, physical healing or personal accomplishments.

Setbacks, disappointments or failure make us stop expecting His promises to be fulfilled in our life, but I want to encourage everyone reading this today that it's never too late! A good example of this truth is seen in the story of Joshua and Caleb. Both men were disappointed when they reached the border of the Promised Land and were unable to enter because the rest of the children of Israel were afraid and didn't believe in God's promises.

They labored, believed and dreamed about seeing the promise fulfilled, but sometimes other people get in the way of God's promises manifesting. In the natural it looked like that was true for Joshua and Caleb; it seemed that their opportunity had passed them by, but with God it's never too late. The bible says God's promises are always "yea and amen"!

It looked like and it felt like it was too late in the natural for them, so therefore.....it was too late. But with God, nothing is impossible; with God, nothing is too late. Though they continued to wander in the wilderness, God removed the obstacles so His promise to them could be fulfilled. It was only after the first generation of Israelites perished that God could bring Joshua and Caleb into the Promised Land.

You may feel like you're too old now, or too much time has passed to see this thing fulfilled. Don't fret, God will renew your youth (as He did for Caleb and Joshua) so you can enjoy your hopes and dreams. Read the list below and remember, with God it's never too late!

Answer this question. Did God drop those desires and passions in your heart or were they just a work of your own emotions and intellect? If God put them there, trust Him to fulfill them no matter what. It's impossible for God to lie or break His promises. So take the limits off and know it's never too late when God's in it.

Do some things have to be removed from your life before God's promise can come to pass? For God's promise to be fulfilled, Abraham had to remove his mistake..... Ishmael was interfering with the promise that was meant to be fulfilled in Isaac. Is the Ishmael in your life holding back God's promise, causing you to think it's too late? One reason your hope hasn't been fulfilled yet, is that God is getting rid of your Ishmaels (works of the flesh).

The issue could be timing. Jacob was meant to get Isaac's birthright, but instead of waiting for God's timing he took it into his own hands. (By the way, God's timing is to prepare us to be good stewards over the blessings.) Jacob stole the birthright prematurely and it nearly cost him his life. Timing is everything when it comes to God's promises, so don't give up on the blessings, no matter what disappointments or failures you've experienced. God knows how to get His blessings to you on time.... and at the right time. It's never too late.

Know this; the devil can't steal God's blessings without your cooperation. By letting your disappointments and past failures cause you stop believing the best is ahead, you're cooperating with Satan. Remember.... With God, it's never too late!

▍ Your Life is a Movie

There are certain components that have to be in place to make any movie a success. These components are a collection of interesting and clearly defined scenes and the intended length of the movie will determine the number of scenes. To express the whole purpose of the movie there also needs to be a clearly defined ending.

Let me give you an example: An old man on a park bench was reading a newspaper when a young man sat next to him. The young man turned to the older gentleman and said, "Sir, do you happen to have the time?"

The older man very abruptly said, "No!" The younger man noticed he had a watch on his wrist and followed up with a question, "Sir, did I offend you in anyway?" The older man said to him again in an abrupt manner, "No!" The young man couldn't let it go so he asked another question, "Sir, I noticed you have a watch on your wrist. Why wouldn't you tell me the time?"

The old man turned himself around, faced him this time and replied, "Son, if I told you the time, we would engage in a conversation and I would probably have gotten to like you. I would have then proceeded to invite you over for dinner where you would have met my beautiful, unmarried daughter. You would probably have asked her out for date and most likely the two of you would have fallen in love. You would have asked me for her hand in marriage, but quite frankly son, I wouldn't want my daughter to marry some-body who couldn't afford a watch."

This is a funny story but it illustrates my point of how life is like a movie. The old man looked at the first scene and based on the likely ending, decided he wasn't going to even start a conversation with the young man.

If you know how the story is going to end, you can adjust the scenes to ensure that your ending is the way you want it. On our last blog about making a life plan I quoted that, "to fail to plan will lead you to plan to fail." Your life is a movie and you can adjust each scene to make sure you get the desired ending.

Decide what you desire your ending to be like.

Review the scenes of your life to make sure they line up with what you want your ending to be. This will affect every decision you make.

Constantly ask the question, "Will this be something I want in my life movie? Will it lead to the ending I believe for and I am plan-ning for?"

Be courageous; remove any scene in your movie that will con-tradict the grand finale.

Overcoming Fear, Grief & Disappointment

▌ Identifying Signs of Depression

E very day millions of people (especially young people) are bat- tling depression and they don't even know it. Depression can be caused by many things, but let's take a look at some of the causes:

Loss: of a loved one, job, longtime friendship, confidence, etc.

Failure: such as a marriage, your dream or vision, career, etc.

Stress: to succeed, to be liked by everybody, to perform at an acceptable level required by peers, etc.

Blood lines: depression can be passed down through the genes from one generation to another.

Whatever the cause may be, if it goes undetected in your life you'll function at a low level of performance in every area. It's like dragging around a 100 lb. weight, affecting your sex drive, work performance, social life and just plain old everyday living. Eventu- ally you adjust the way you conduct your daily business just to make it through the day.

I could go into detail about some symptoms such as feelings of inadequacy and hopelessness; difficulty sleeping or sleeping too much; thoughts of dying and attempting suicide; extreme weight gain or loss; and not being able to concentrate (a very common symptom). But I prefer to spend the rest of our time giving you God's remedy for depression. Here they are:

Debrief: Before you go to bed take 15 minutes to make a list of the most stressful things in your life and then follow the directions in Philippians 4:6-8, "Be anxious for nothing, but in everything by prayer and supplication, with thanksgiving, let your requests be made known to God; and the peace of God, which surpasses all understanding, will guard your hearts and minds through Christ Jesus. Finally, brethren, whatever things are true, whatever things are noble, whatever things are just, whatever things are pure, whatever things are lovely, whatever things are of good report, if there is any virtue and if there is anything praiseworthy—meditate on these things." This practice will assure you will have peace and protection over your mind, leading to a good night's sleep. That habit will overflow into the next day.

Thanksgiving: This seems simple and inconsequential, but when consistently implemented it will transform your perception of yourself and allow God to fulfill His destiny for you. Practice giving thanksgiving three times a day, (set your phone alarm as a reminder). Take just a minute or two first thing in the morning, mid-day and right after dinner to thank God for all your blessings. 1 Thessalonians 5:18 says, "In everything give thanks; for this is the will of God in Christ Jesus for you."

Thank Him that He has given you the gift of life; placed certain people around you; sustained and provided for you; and most important He sent Jesus to redeem you from eternal damnation. This habit invites God into your 24 hour day and we know that wherever God is….. Satan and his works (depression) must flee.

Be "otherly": Go out of your way each day to find one person you can be a blessing to. Bless them with kind deeds and acts of mercy such as praying for them or doing something to make their day easier. This allows God's love to flow out of your spirit, making it whole and healthy. When your spirit is healthy, your whole being will be. Proverbs 4:23 says, "Keep your heart with all diligence, For out of it spring the issues of life."

Conclusion: doing these few exercises consistently will deliver you from depression. I know the world says to take medication or go to a psychiatrist to deal with depression. But God is smarter than anyone in the world. Isn't it time that we start trusting in the God who made us? He knows how to fix us!

▍ Six Steps to Overcoming Fear

1 **Be Careful What You Hear.** Romans 10:17 says, "Faith comes by hearing" and just like faith, the same is true with fear. What you hear will either cause you to trust God more or cause you to doubt Him. Once you doubt God, you will trust in what you see with your natural eyes and hear with your natural ears.

Think about the people who speak into your life. Do their words increase your already existing fear?

Assess what you watch on TV, the internet and read in books. Your ears (and eyes) are gateways for fear or faith. What you allow to enter into your spirit is your choice!

2. Know For Sure That God Loves You. He is with you and it is His will that you overcome fear. If this truth is secure in your heart it will make all the difference. Read the Word to see how much He loves you and what He has done to prove it to you. Faith (the opposite of fear) won't be activated unless God's love is secure in your heart. Galatians 5:6b, ".......faith working through love."

3. Walk in God's Love. Imitate Jesus' love to everyone you struggle with, especially those you hold un-forgiveness towards. 1 John 4:18a says, "There is no fear in love; but perfect love (God's love) casts out fear, because fear involves torment." When you forgive those who hurt you and love your enemies; you are defeating the spirit of fear and guarding your heart from future fear entering in.

4. Stop Backing Off And Start Living. Fear causes you to pull back and even become a recluse. The devil loves to set false boundaries to control you and keep you away from God's best. Resist those boundaries of fear and trust in God. He is with you and will never leave you. To begin this step, resist your natural feelings, trust in God's word and depend on the Holy Spirit for help. He will give you the confidence to break out of the false boundaries. Progress always involves risk but take some Holy Ghost risks: love again, trust again, reach out again, dream again!

5. Elevate Your Mind Above What You See. See what God sees about your circumstances and life; not what the devil shows you in the natural. What you see today is changeable, but God's word is forever. Get rid of the double vision and choose to see what God sees. It will eventually become a life style; it's worth the effort.

6. Avoid Anxiety. Your adversary wants to worry you to death! Anxiety opens the doors for fear to control your life. Most of our worries won't happen so avoid anxiety and close the door on fear. Philippians 4:6 tells us, "be anxious for nothing but in everything with prayer and supplication with thanksgiving let your request be made known to God."

Conclusion: A fearful Christian (F=false, E=evidence, A=appearing, R=real) is not an option. In Matthew 6:25-34 Jesus told His disciples to fear not. Fear waters down faith and opens the doorway for Satan to invade us with fear but God's will is that we choose to live by faith and not live in fear.

What to Do with Disappointment (part 1)

Everyone in life will face some kind of a disappointment from time to time, because it's part of life itself. But, not everybody handles disappointment with success. For many of us, disappointments control us, overtaking our feelings, emotions, and decisions....leading us to live a life filled with hopelessness and despair.

There are 5 important truths to keep in mind when facing the disappointments in life. Understanding these truths will change our mindset forever, so let's take a brief look at them:

1. Disappointment is a weapon Satan uses to steal the dream and vision that God placed in our heart. His primary goal is to make us quit believing and expecting those God-inspired dreams and visions to actually come to pass. Remember how Joseph's prophetic dreams caused his brothers to get so angry that they wanted to kill him? Why? Because Satan was using them to stop Joseph the dreamer from giving birth to those dreams. Satan really isn't after you directly, but he wants to destroy the dream God gave you. He knows that when you begin to actually walk out your dreams, you will be extremely dangerous to him and his strategies to defeat you. Joseph eventually was used by God to save His chosen people. If you remember that the disappointment you face isn't directly against you, but against God's destiny for you, it will give you greater determination to not give in or be controlled by disappointment. James 1:1-3

2. Disappointments give you an opportunity to stand back and evaluate what you are disappointed about. Is it really from God? Many of us have godly ideas and thoughts of what we want to see happen in our lives, but not all godly dreams and visions are for us personally. They may be wholesome and seem to have great potential to bring success in your life. But if they are not from God, (not engrafted into your spirit) they will cause you to waste valuable time. You will be constantly caught in the same cycles of disappointment over and over again for the same things. Allow the disappointment to give you the chance to take a second look to see if what you are hoping for is from God.

3. Experiencing some failure in life doesn't mean that the dream, vision, or prophetic word that God engrafted in your heart is wrong. Many times it's a sign that the strategy needs to be changed. Ex: God spoke to me about taking back America, one city at a time. So I decided that Sarasota, which was about an hour and a half away from our church, would be the place to start. After about six months I became disappointed because there wasn't much fruit. The Lord told me my vision for America is correct, but my strategy was wrong. So, I immediately stopped the work in Sarasota, followed God's strategy and very quickly I experienced awesome fruitfulness.

Conclusion: I'll continue speaking more about strategy and the rest of the truths concerning disappointment on Monday. I believe that by understanding these truths, your life will change. Remember, not all disappointments are focused on God's dream and vision in our life. Some are because we don't have any direction from God, and some disappointments come because we are following our own lustful desires. Proverbs 14:12 says, "There is a way that seems right to a man, But its end is the way of death." You were created for God's purposes…. not your own. Find out what God has planned for the "reason of your being"; when you do, disappointment will never win in your life again.

What to Do with Disappointment (part 2)

As I mentioned in my previous blog, disappointment can become a way of life for us. It's easy to learn to expect and even accept disappointments to happen regularly, but this mindset sabotages us and can eventually lead to depression, sadness and hopelessness taking hold of our life.

Let's add to the three truths we learned so far:

4. Disappointment is one of Satan's weapons but it can be resisted. It can be resisted if we are willing to recognize it and then engage in this high level of spiritual warfare. James 4:7 says we must submit ourselves to God AND resist the devil (come out against him).

We need to be aggressively on the offense, not on the defense. In the Greek, resist comes from the word antihistamine, which is how our bodies fight allergies. But, how do we offensively fight disappointment? Glad you asked, because God gave us a weapon to defeat disappointment every time.

Remember, Satan uses disappointment to rob the dream, prophetic word and/or promise God gave us. That word fills us with the faith to expect God's destiny to be fulfilled…. It gets us up in the morning and encourages us to "keep on keepin' on" when all hell's breaking out.

That word is a spiritual weapon and when you speak it against the mountain of disappointment, it will be defeated. Jesus taught this truth to His disciples in Matthew 17:20 and Mark 11:22&23.

When you speak the engrafted word that the Holy Spirit has birthed in your heart, you're releasing God's presence and power. Prophecy your destiny (calling the end from the beginning) by speaking that engrafted word, and don't let the devil talk you out of it. God is sovereign, but your destiny won't come to pass until you release what God planted in your heart.

5. Step into your God-given destiny. After releasing the prophetic word God gave you, you must guard against the temptation to not go forward and pursue your dream. Although he was 100 and Sarah was 90, to fulfill God's promise of being the father of many nations, Abraham still had to be intimate with Sarah.

If God gave a word to you about your career, marriage, ministry, your family or even a vacation; don't just speak it.....pursue it with all your heart! Don't let any obstacle stand in your way. Years ago, I remember planning a long-overdue vacation that had been in my heart for quite a while. We packed the car with enough clothes for a week, but there was one problem; we had no money! I'd been prophesying to the mountain of disappointment and finally made my mind up to pursue it. That would seem ridiculous to most people, but God said He would provide for the dream He placed in me.

As we drove off for vacation, the woman behind me kept beeping her horn until I recognized it was one of my congregants. I pulled over to see what was wrong and this dear woman said, "Pastor, God told me to give you this money. I don't know what it's for, but He told me you needed it." Well, as you can imagine, it more than covered my family vacation!

Conclusion: Speak your destiny into existence.....then step into your miracle! The Holy Spirit planted God's word for your destiny in your heart. Receive that engrafted word in your heart

as your top priority. Remember you and God make a majority.....
disappointment doesn't ever have to be a way of life again!

Strengthening Your Relationship with God

▌ Barging in on God

have been pastoring a local church now for over thirty years and have consistently maintained office hours for my congregation. I was always available for appointments a minimum of five days a week, eight hours a day and whenever necessary.

I had a hard time dealing with people who would barge in on me as though their issue was the only thing that was on my mind. Although I was never rude or short with anyone, I felt that they should follow the proper protocol.

We all know that to stay healthy and functioning we need to follow some kind of protocol. Our body needs to be fed a few times a day and it requires at least five or six hours of sleep a day.

We like to have protocol in our life and don't like it when people barge in on our routine. But, the good news is that God's not like us! He invites us to barge in on Him whether it's an emergency or not!

He actually loves it when we interrupt Him to meet our needs. Unlike us humans, He never gets tired and He doesn't need a bathroom break. Psalm 121:4, "Behold, He who keeps Israel Shall neither slumber nor sleep." So God gives us an invitation to barge in on Him whenever we want. Psalm 46:1, "God is our refuge and strength, A very present help in trouble."

The following thoughts will help you remember that it is okay to interrupt and barge in on God:

1) Don't look at Him as just a super-human being. He is God and He has no beginning and no end. He has no limits.

2) Don't allow Satan to make you feel unworthy or inferior so you say things like, "I don't want to bother God with my problems. He has more important issues than mine."

3) Remember, God invites us to barge in on Him. It is God's will that we interrupt Him with the littlest need. Luke 9:10, ""So I say to you, ask, and it will be given to you; seek, and you will find; knock, and it will be opened to you. "For everyone who asks receives, and he who seeks finds, and to him who knocks it will be opened. "

4) You aren't a bother to God. He doesn't respond just because we are good or not respond because we are being bad.

Philippians 4:19, "And my God shall supply all your need according to His riches in glory by Christ Jesus."

★★Don't let Satan trick you. ....It's okay to barge in on God. Start right now and receive the blessings that God wants to pour out on you!

God's Grace In Our Cycles and Seasons

Everything in life has cycles and seasons, as we are told in Genesis 8:22, " While the earth remains, seedtime and harvest, cold and heat, winter and summer, and day and night shall not cease." Recognizing where you are in life's cycle will give you an advantage over Satan. Why? Because there are certain things you can and can't do in certain cycles. Knowing the grace God has for you is the key in all of this, but it's important to recognize that His grace comes in many different ways. Let me list of a few ways that God's grace can be working in our life.

Through desires and passions: The Holy Spirit will place desires and passions that weren't there before to accomplish God's will in your life. For instance, He will rekindle a desire to work on your marriage, lose weight, overcome bad habits or addictions, change careers, press into God more, etc. They can be things you always wanted to do, but you just never could. But, now you see that God placed those desires and passions in you and He also gave you the grace to accomplish His will.

Through divine appointments: Someone suddenly comes into your life, seemingly out of nowhere and you see that they're a good influence; encouraging you to do things that are right in the sight of God. For instance, you connect with an old friend you haven't seen in years and learn that they're on fire for Jesus! By connecting with them again, you're encouraged to re-commit yourself to a stronger walk with God. Or, you make friends with a co-worker who has a great marriage and family life, so now you decide it's time to put your marriage and family first. These aren't coincidences; they're by design and are proof of God's grace for this season.

Through unexpected trouble: It sound strange, but many times God allows trouble in our life so we'll change our current course and realign it with His plans for us. Maybe we've been comfortable in our job for years and wouldn't think of changing, but, because God wants to give us a better job with more influence for His kingdom, trouble comes and we are forced to leave. Or perhaps God's allowing conflict in certain friendships because they aren't beneficial to us and are actually keeping us from fulfilling His purpose. In fact, these relationships may be the very thing holding back God's blessings.

These are just a few of the ways that God's grace is released. They can help us to recognize the season we're in..... a time we can accomplish things to align us with His plans and destiny. This grace is not just coincidental; it's God's divine intervention in our life. They are His open doors and if we walk through them by yielding to Him, we will accomplish life changes we've struggled with in the past. We will do things we always knew were right, but could never succeed by our own will power.

Everyone goes through life cycles and seasons. Don't miss your great victory by not recognizing God's grace to do what you could never do yourself. Start looking for His grace in your life and focus on that area, knowing that every cycle and season has a beginning and an end. You don't want to miss the opportunity to accomplish things you know you can't do on your own, because you'll have to wait for that cycle to return again. God's grace is just for that season, so enjoy your God-given opportunity for victory and success!

▍ How Big Is Your God?

n Isaiah 6:1, when the prophet saw the Lord high and lifted up and the train of His robe filling the temple, he gained fresh revelation of the awesome power and authority God really has. He was overwhelmed by this vision of God! You see, in Isaiah's day, kings attached to their train, the trains of kings they defeated in battle. The length of the train indicated the authority of that king, so Isaiah described his revelation of the one and only true God as a king with unlimited power and authority!

Our fears, frustrations, depression and hopelessness come from a lack of revelation of how big and awesome our God truly is. The God we identify with determines the amount of fear, stress, worry and hopelessness we experience. If we see God the way Isaiah did, opposition won't make us afraid or discouraged.

We must never stop desiring deeper understanding of what God can do in and through our lives, because yesterday's revelation won't meet today's challenges. Too many people are living on yesterday's understanding and they're filled with fear, anxiety and worry; a sure sign that the God they identify with is too small.

What God do you identify with; one who is able to do this.... but not that? Remember, Isaiah was already God's prophet before he received that new revelation. If he needed to be reminded of who God really is, how much more do we need a fresh download of revelation from heaven?

Here are some ways to increase your revelation of how authoritative and powerful your God really is:

It takes brokenness, demonstrated by meekness and humility. We can't expect to get fresh revelation if we are prideful, self-righteous or un-teachable. Isaiah was devastated by the death of the friend and king he served for 52 years. But, through his devastation he glimpsed the True King. The removal of people we put before God or a devastating experience will often bring us to that point of humility and brokenness.

We need a desire to know God more. Some people are satisfied with what they already know of God. They stop pursuing Him, but God only feeds the hungry. Ask God to give you a deeper hunger for more of Him. He'll certainly answer that prayer, because He wants to be known, revealing Himself to those seeking Him with all their heart. Moses served God for many years, but when he cried out to know Him more, he experienced His presence to the point that God's glory shone from his face!

Let's seek Him with all our heart: People always say they love God with all their heart, but they're deceived if God isn't their main passion. The acid test is, what do you do when no one is watching? Do you spend time just loving on Him? Is He the focus of your attention? Jeremiah 29:12-14a, "Then you will call upon Me and go and pray to Me, and I will listen to you. And you will seek Me and find Me, when you search for Me with all your heart. I will be found by you, says the Lord...." The key phrase is, with all your heart. Plead with God to turn your heart to Him and no one else.

Like Isaiah, we need to acknowledge we have "unclean lips". Isaiah knew his language revealed a lack of understanding of how big God really is. Change what you say to your mountain....stop agreeing with your problems and stop complaining about what God isn't doing in your life. God's power is in His word, so if your God is big enough; your words ought to reflect that. How big your God is will be revealed by the words you speak.

▌ Stop Eating Junk Food

am sure we all remember our mother telling us to stop eating junk food during the day because it would ruin our appetite for dinner. We loved to gorge ourselves on potato chips, pretzels and Snicker Bars throughout the day. By the time we came home to eat the dinner our mom worked hard to prepare, we had no appetite left! Eating food without nutritional temporarily filled us, but always left us feeling unsatisfied.

Well, the same thing holds true with our hunger for God. When was the last time you experienced a real hunger for more of God in your life? It's sad to say but most Christians have lost their hunger for Him because they've been filling themselves with the wrong food. ....they're full but not satisfied. What kind of Sunday service would it be if there was a building full of people who were hungry for more of God?

Let me give you a hint, based on firsthand experience. First of all, everyone would enter corporate praise and worship with a heart to pursue God's presence. It wouldn't be church as usual that day! Instead of the worship team trying to pump up and motivate people who just want to be entertained, pride and self-preservation would be gone and there would be a building filled with self-abandoned worshipers! Of course, this scenario makes religious people feel very uncomfortable, because the fear of losing control and making a fool of themselves trumps their inner desire for God's presence.

Do you know what that kind of hunger really feels like? Most of us have had momentary bouts of hunger, but few really know the hunger that drives you to abandon everything else to satisfy those deep hunger pains. That's who Jesus was describing in Matthew 5:6, "blessed are those that hunger and thirst after righteousness for they shall be filled" Jesus said that being hungry for God is a blessed condition to be in!

We're missing that hunger and have lost our appetite for more of God in today's church because of all the junk food we've been eating. What is the junk food? We've been reading books about God instead of His word, spending more time watching TV than praying; substituting going to church instead of being the church; measuring spiritual growth and maturity by our knowledge about the word instead of how much we know about the author of the word. We're hearers of the word, not doers and we aren't seeing His presence being manifested in our everyday lives. I'm sure you could identify more junk food that's taking away our appetite.

But, God is faithful to put a hunger for more of Him through circumstance, or troubles, or just one blessing after another that comes our way. If we don't respond to that hunger, we'll lose it in just a few days because, like hunger pains in the natural, after a while they eventually go away if they are ignored.

Conclusion: God is once again putting a hunger in all of our hearts because of the season we live in. Without more of Him we won't fulfill our call to be the light and the salt of the earth so let's get rid of the junk food! It's taken away our appetite and just left us weak and unsatisfied. The apostle Paul had clearly expressed his hunger for more of God in Philippians 3:14, "I press (aggressively) toward the goal for the prize of the upward call of God in Christ Jesus." If we don't already have it, let's commit to pray for God to give us a hunger for more of Him, and let's show our hunger by relentlessly pursing Him individually and corporately. His manifest presence is everything!

▌ We Need His Presence

Today I see many people, Christians or not, suffering terribly…and much of their suffering is not of their own doing. One thing the world and our religion have in common- they both don't have the answer to this epidemic of increasing human suffering! You'd think that the bible- believing churchgoers would be exempt from these things, but when you compare the two, sadly there's no marked difference.

There are the same numbers of people who are sick, divorced, poverty-stricken, angry, jealous, fearful, depressed and dying before their time who go to church, as those who don't! So, something is radically wrong with the church today, because 1 John 5:4&5 tells me believers should be world overcomers, "For whatever is born of God overcomes the world. And this is the victory that has overcome the world—our faith. Who is he who overcomes the world, but he who believes that Jesus is the Son of God?" In other words, we're equipped to be victorious over the things I stated above.

So, what's wrong? It's very simple; we lack the tangible presence of God! From the Old to the New Testament, whenever God's tangible presence showed up….pain, sickness and suffering left. Not some of the time; all of the time. I conclude that God's presence is the only answer to today's ever-increasing human suffering.

The church is supposed to be the source of His presence and offer hope to a suffering, dying world. We need an immediate spiritual makeover! Our mistaken idea is that church is all about us, when in fact…. it's all about Him! We come to church for handouts and spiritual highs, but the truth is, we were set apart as God's priesthood to worship and honor Him.

True worship is a fragrance that attracts and releases His tangible presence in our midst. When God's glory (His presence) is released, it destroys every work of Satan. Don't get me wrong, God wants to meet our needs and make us feel good, but He wants much more for us. He wants us to walk in His divine health and prosperity, carrying His tangible presence to the world.

Friends; God is placing a hunger and thirst in our hearts to desire His manifest presence. Many of us are fed up with being sick, broke, hurt, living in poverty and having broken relationships. We've had it with "church as usual", lacking the power to change this world. We want and need His presence! I don't know about you, but I joined up to be His true church….. that's not possible without the manifestation of God's tangible presence.

God's word repeatedly says, return to Him and He will return (release His manifest, tangible presence) to us. If, like me, you have a holy dissatisfaction and want His presence back in His church again, here's a few things that are making a difference in my walk with God.

1. I ask God every day to fill me with a hunger and thirst for His tangible presence in my life.

2. I set aside a few times daily to pursue His presence through worship, prayer (in the spirit) and godly declarations.

3. I try to walk in the fear (honor, reverence, respect) of the Lord. I seek His advice, counsel and direction in everything I do, asking what He would have me do in any given situation. This makes me more aware of God's interaction in my life and helps me to be less self-centered and self-sufficient.

4. I expect God's tangible presence to flow through my life daily.

5. I no longer look at corporate gatherings (church) as a time to meet my needs, but as a time to bless and worship God and meet His needs. His need is to tangibly show up in our midst. "Seek ye first the kingdom of God and His righteousness and everything else shall be added unto you."

Friends, we need His presence and He's longing for us to desire Him more than life itself. When He shows up, everything changes for the better. Let's pray like Moses when he asked....Lord, show me Your glory!

You Can Have as Much of God as You Want

n yesterday's blog about our need for God's presence, I stated that He desires His presence to be made known to us and the world we live in. John 1:14a says, "And the Word became flesh and dwelt among us, and we beheld His glory," Since creation, when God walked in the Garden with Adam and Eve until today, God has always made Himself available to us and has desired to tabernacle (tangibly dwell) with us.

Throughout the bible, God cries out for us to return to Him and He will return to us. He beckons us to call upon Him, seek Him, pursue Him and He will be found. He consistently encourages us to replace our religious concept of God with glory of His manifest presence.

Today, God's once again calling to you and me, making Himself available… not just to live in us, but to be seen and experienced in, through and around us. How can we experience this phenomenal invitation by Almighty God, the Creator of all things? By yearning for His manifest presence in our lives. Here are a few things God says about this subject.

1. The theme in Proverbs 8:17 is repeated over and over, "I love those who love me, (love my presence) And those who seek me diligently will find me.".** God isn't hiding; but we need to examine our motives for wanting His presence. He's waiting for us to express our desire for Him before He will reveal Himself in a tangible way.

Jeremiah 29:13 clarifies this even more," And you will seek Me and find Me, when you search for Me with all your heart." The key is "with all your heart" (passion, desire).

2. How badly do you want His manifest presence and what are you willing to do (or not) to welcome Him? Those are legitimate questions to answer in order to have as much of God's presence as you want. He's available to us, but we determine how much of Him we can have.

After experiencing God's tangible presence, David couldn't live without it, so he cried out in Psalm 51:11, "Do not cast me away from Your presence, And do not take Your Holy Spirit from me." God didn't hold His presence back, because He was attracted to the worship that came from David's humble and meek heart.

God places that hunger and thirst in us in various ways. Sometimes He allows disappointments, so we will turn to Him. Or, sometimes He reveals Himself in such an amazing way, that nothing else satisfies us. Once we've experienced Him like that it ruins us; mere religion doesn't do it for us anymore.

I tell you, my friends; the answer to your problem isn't found in a bottle, a pill, a divorce or even more money...it's in God's manifest presence. I'm on a personal mission to seek Him with all my heart and, for as long as God gives me life, carry His presence wherever I go.

Years ago, when I first gave my life to Jesus, I made a commitment that if He's truly God and the bible's really His word, I'll pursue Him and live according to His word. That commitment holds true even more today because of the many times He's shown Himself in a tangible way in my life.

When John Wesley was asked why so many people came and were saved at his meetings, he said, "I get passionately on fire for God and people come and watch me burn!"

This world is in great trouble and only God's manifest presence will set people free and deliver their souls from hell. Let's make the necessary choices and sacrifices, and desire more of God's tangible presence. It's our privilege, honor and call as true Christians to host His presence. My prayer for you and me is that we would live the rest of our lives in pursuit of more of Him!

Improving Your Personal Relationships

Forgiveness: The Breakfast of Champions

When we decide that we want to live a healthy life, the first thing we examine is our eating habits. And of course we start with the most important meal: breakfast!

Everyone knows that if we start the day off right, most often than not it will also end right. Therefore, what we eat for breakfast needs to come under close scrutiny. If we want to see an improvement, we begin to make quality decisions by eliminating certain foods to achieve our desired goal.

This same principle applies to living a healthy spiritual life as well. We must choose to let go of any spiritual "junk food" such as: anger, resentment, hatred, retaliation, etc. all of which are by-products of having unforgiveness in our life.

Too many of us enjoy a steady diet of unforgiveness for break-fast every day, but we MUST change our old diet and adopt a new one…. starting with breakfast (which means to break our fast from the night before).

Imagine the spiritual effects of starting every day with an unhealthy breakfast of unforgiveness? It's like putting a little poison in our natural food for breakfast every day! The toxins ultimately build up, destroy our physical health and lead to sickness and an early death.

Well, the same is true in the spiritual sense. If we continuously feed on the poison of un-forgiveness, it distorts our perception of God, others, ourselves and even our view of our circumstances.

Athletic champions are empowered by a passion for success and they're willing to make the tough choices it takes to fulfill their goals. They don't just talk the talk…. they also walk the walk!

These champions diligently watch what they eat, refusing to defile themselves by indulging in the pleasantries and the "junk food" of life. They're focused on staying healthy so they can accomplish their goals.

Certainly, as champions of the faith, we need to do the same thing by passionately desiring to be successful in our Christian walk. Our passion gives us the determination to eliminate unforgiveness from our diet. Every day should start with an attitude of forgiveness, because forgiveness will fortify our spirit and make us "unoffendable."

Forgiveness means to decide ahead of time (for/before time) to give mercy to those who have stepped on our toes. It's not meant to be a last minute struggle to make the decision to forgive or not forgive.

To the champions of the faith; forgiveness is a lifestyle, their daily breakfast….a great way to start off the day!

Here's some ways to eat the breakfast of champions.

Guard against those who want to fill your heart with gossip. Don't be someone else's garbage bin; tell them to take their garbage to Jesus, not you.

Guard your own lips. Don't let poison spew out of them.

Resolve conflicts with others right away. Don't allow your heart to get bitter. Choose to have an unoffendable heart.

Every conflict won't get resolved right away, so don't hold things in your heart if issues don't get settled immediately. Instead, pray for the people who hurt you and your heart will stay soft towards God and them.

Finally, have the right perception of what you're going through. Recognize that God's working things out in your life. Ask Him what He wants you to see or do in the situation.

Remember, you are God's champion. So make sure you eat a "champion of the faith" breakfast daily!

▌ Double Vision

Have you ever experienced double vision in your life? You may have had it because of some trauma to your head, dizziness or just because you have poor eyesight. Whatever the cause, double vision is very troubling because you are seeing two things at the same time. You don't know what is real and what is only an illusion.

If you're not already dizzy, double vision will create dizziness. It affects every aspect of your life such as driving, working, playing.... you can't function at all! It's not fun to live with double vision.

Thank God there is a remedy today for anyone suffering from double vision in the natural realm. Obviously the goal of every remedy for double vision is to give them single vision. Single vision means seeing one thing at a time and knowing what is real instead of confusing it with an illusion. It's very disconcerting to not know what to believe or not believe.

Well, in the Spirit realm many of us have double vision concerning our beliefs. We don't accurately see God's spiritual blessings (Ephesians 1:3). We partially see what the word says and at the same time partially see what our circumstances tell us.

As long as we have double vision we can't receive what God has for us. Hebrews 11:6 says it is impossible for us to please God without faith. Well, faith is seeing what God sees about our life through His word, but double vision prevents us from seeing our lives clearly through God's word.

Double vision will delay (if not completely hinder) your blessing from God. If you see that "by Jesus Christ's stripes you are healed" but at the same time you see and believe the doctor's report that you are very sick, you have double vision.

Here are some things you can do about it

1. Discover what the word of God says about your circumstance. Be accurate in your interpretation by finding it in more than one place in the bible. God's word says, "out of the mouth of two or three witnesses let My Word be established".

2. Determine to believe God's word over what your circumstances want you to see. 2 Corinthians 4:18, "while we do not look at the things which are seen, but at the things which are not seen. For the things which are seen are temporary, but the things which are not seen are eternal."

3. Declare God's Word over your life , not what your natural circumstance show you. Your confessions will increase your faith to see God's Word as reality and not illusion.

4. Double vision will try to bring you into confusion daily if you allow it to. I said if YOU allow it to. How you want to see your life today is ultimately your choice.

Conclusion: Double vision causes you to live in doubt and unbelief so go to Dr. Jesus for an eye checkup. He can put the right lenses in your eyes and help you see life through His eyes rather than yours or the ones Satan wants you to look through. Don't live another day with double vision… it will lead you down the wrong road.

The Gift of Goodbye

People come and go in our lives. Sure, some stay longer than others, but we need to recognize that not everyone is tied to our destiny. I believe the latter group consists of the people who are no longer with us. God may have connected them to us for a season and they may have even helped us get to where we are today. But, they were not tied to our destiny.

That is why everybody needs to receive and operate in what I call the "10th spiritual gift, the gift of goodbye!" The Apostle John recognized this and we read in 1 John 2:19, "They went out from us, but they were not of us; for if they had been of us, they would have continued with us; but they went out that they might be made manifest, that none of them were of us."

If someone is no longer with us; we need to practice that 10th spiritual gift but too often, we do everything we can to convince them to stay with us, or love us, or visit us etc. But, if after we have tried everything and they still walk out on us, we need to let them walk.... They're not tied to our destiny. God allowed them to separate and maybe He was the one who actually removed them from us.

People tied to our destiny aren't easily discouraged when things get tough in our life because they're willing to honor their covenant relationship with us, come hell or high water! In the Book of Ruth, Naomi's daughter-in-law Orpah left her after many years and returned to her own family. This didn't make her a bad person; she just wasn't appointed to share Naomi's destiny. On the other hand, Ruth was the one called to share Naomi's destiny, so she left her comfort zone and followed Naomi to Bethlehem.

People who have left us are not evil and they are not our enemy, so we need to be careful to not make rash judgments about them. Not understanding this, we often label these people and speak negative things about them because they're gone. This critical response creates division in the church.

Instead, once we recognize they are not tied to our future, we need to exercise the "gift of goodbye" and completely release them into their own destiny. If we don't say goodbye and remain focused on convincing them to stay, we may actually miss the very people God has sent to walk the journey with us!

I have written down some points to help you determine who is and who isn't tied to your destiny.

They don't share your destiny if:

They lose interest in the things that interest you.

They are hard to get hold of, backing away from the friendship you once had.

They begin to criticize you and may even talk bad about you.

They suddenly and completely remove themselves from your life.

They do share your destiny if:

They have stuck with you despite your weaknesses and failures.

They come quickly and consistently to your defense in the troubled times of your life.

They are great encouragers when everyone else has bailed out on you.

Every one of us has people that have been appointed to share our destiny. Find them and then celebrate them because they are true gifts from God. Concerning the others, learn to let go and graciously say goodbye. But be sure to keep on loving them; for this is the will of God!

▌ How to Confront

'm sure you will agree that most people hate confrontation and will do anything to avoid it. And when push comes to shove and they're forced to confront, it usually ends up being a negative experience. This pattern leads to the ungodly belief that it's better to just avoid conflicts than to confront them, but that is not the truth.

Unresolved conflicts create anger, which leads to bitterness in our hearts against the people who offended us. Unresolved conflicts will ultimately poison our marriages, friendships, church relationships and even our employer and employee relationships.

Matthew 18:15 and other scriptures strongly exhort us to resolve all the conflicts in our relationships through confrontation, "Moreover if your brother sins against you, go and tell him his fault between you and him alone. If he hears you, you have gained your brother."

Here are a few steps that help me to confront those who have hurt me. Remember, because we are relationship-driven, life will always present conflicts that hurt us. But, learning to confront the biblical way will help us have healthier and more successful relationships.

Have the right motives. What is your goal in confronting the other person? Is it to show that you're right and they're wrong? Is it to hurt them like they hurt you? Is it to control, intimidate, humiliate and dominate them? Our goal must be bigger than our personal differences. Our motive should be to love and honor them because they are as valuable and precious to God as we are. Our motive should be to save our relationship and identify stumbling blocks that are in the way. The right motive will determine your success, so allow the Holy Spirit to reveal selfish or faulty motives in your heart before you confront.

We must own the problem. Since reconciliation and the restoration of unity is the goal, we must involve ourselves in the solution to the conflict. What can you do differently to help the other person not react the same way? Even if that person's response was absolutely wrong, find a way to help them overcome their bad reactions. Listening to them, acknowledging their feelings and correcting their misperception of your intentions will go a long way to resolve that conflict. Empathize with their emotions and avoid being defensive or assigning blame. Now, here is the biggest part of owning the problem…. apologize and ask forgiveness for your part of the disagreement! This will open the door for the other person to acknowledge their wrong as well and reciprocate by asking forgiveness from you.

Speak the right words. Make sure your words aren't condemning, blame-shifting, ridiculing or belittling, but speak words of reconciliation. After all, you want to see this relationship healed. That will disarm Satan, who was at the root of this conflict from the beginning. Remember, that person isn't your enemy. The moment you see the real culprit, you're well on your way to resolving the conflict. Words salted with God's love are weapons that destroy Satan's attempt to separate and divide us from one another. Keep a guard over your mouth.

Be a good listener. Listening attentively tells the other person you care, so don't interrupt, but allow them to tell their part of the story. Then ask if they will listen to you, always staying focused on the bigger goal.

Conclusion: Remember, without the Holy Spirit's guidance in all of this we won't accomplish the right results. We need His presence to resolve any conflict, so invite Him into the situation. Before initiating the confrontation, ask the Holy Spirit to empower you to defeat Satan and give you His strategy to resolve the conflict. Don't leave barriers between you and the people God has put in your life. Through confronting, unity is restored and will release God's glory. And that's exactly what we need!

▌ Hurt People Hurt People

The greatest cause of divorce, church splits, family break ups and every kind of broken relationship is "hurt people". What do I mean by hurt people? Hurt people are people with damaged emotions. They have been affected by family issues passed down to them by their ancestors; by hurtful things they experienced in childhood and by their own wrong choices. I know that it's impossible to go through life without some kind pain and suffering, but some people have had more than their share of hurts. These are the people I am classifying as "hurt people".

Hurt people have certain traits in common such as: deep roots of rejection, low self-esteem, inferiority complexes, perfectionism, self-condemnation and a critical and judgmental spirit, to name a few. These ingredients are a recipe for troubled and broken relationships because the individual has an over-emphasized, magnified, self-centered awareness. An easily offended spirit dominates their perception of all the people they interact with.

"Hurt people" hurt people, but not on purpose. The pain they suffer is beyond natural understanding and because they are often misunderstood they suffer rejection, adding to the pain they already carry. They look okay on the outside, so you can't tell how deeply hurt they are by just looking at their physical appearance. It's like the old saying "you can't judge a book by its cover", but when you start reading a few chapters you can size up the whole book pretty quickly.

Hurt people are like time bombs waiting to implode and explode at the first sign of rejection and if there are two hurt people in relationship with each other, it's truly a formula for disaster! It's just a matter of time until they're at odds with each other and they'll eventually separate. Or even worse, they may actually physically hurt each other..... including murder.

If you have deep hurts and are in a relationship as described above, it is very painful and dangerous. Both people are victims of their own hurts so in this type of relationships there are no winners... just losers. The wounds increase and the cycle just continues.

Are you a hurt person? Certain signs can alert you that you are, so here are some identifying signs:

You have had many broken relationships in the past.

You need to control and manipulate your current friends.

You're critical and judgmental of people you are no longer in relationship with (blame-shifting) or who disagree with you.

The people you hang with think like you, so gossip is the foundation of the friendship.

You have fewer and fewer friends and have become more isolated.

Remember, many people carry deep wounds.... you are not alone. Also remember that it wasn't your choice to be hurt, but you can choose to get healed. If you have been deeply wounded, there is something you can do to be set free. It isn't easy to admit how deeply wounded you are, but to fix anything you need to first admit that it's broken.

Here are some suggestions:

For a season, avoid intimate, personal relationships and just work on allowing God to heal you. God is a great physician who can go where no knife can go.

Ask God to heal you from the inside out. He's waiting for you to ask. Without faith you can't receive everything God has already supplied for you.

Make it a priority to stay in God's presence often by reading His word, praying in the Spirit, becoming a worshipper of Him and finally by getting prayer from the Stop Hurting Start Healing ministry. God desires that you live a pain-free life, so take a look at our SHSH website: www. StopHurtingStartHealing.com and make a decision today to stop being a "hurt person" and become a "healed person"!

▌ Know Who Your Real Enemy Is

With the end of this age drawing near and the second coming of Jesus at hand, we are all experiencing an increase in spiritual warfare. The battleground of this war is played out in our mind, so our archenemy Satan's weapon of choice is to try to give us evil thoughts and wicked imaginations. He uses circumstances to stir up thoughts and feelings such as fear, despair, anger, jealousy and depression, to just name a few.

The devil's goal is to tempt you to react impulsively to the thoughts and imaginations he places in your mind. That's the crux of spiritual warfare, but most are clueless to his tactics and strategies, believing they themselves have originated those thoughts and feelings. And if they continue to dwell on these damaging thoughts instead of rejecting them and casting them out of their mind, they'll fall victim to their suggestions and influence.

Know who the real enemy is in your life so you can fulfill the great destiny God created you for. Here are some of the strategies Satan uses against us:

He makes us believe God is against us. He deceives us into thinking that God is holding us back and is against us. If you buy Satan's lie, it takes the focus off him and he can operate covertly in your life. God created you for success and He would never undermine His own plan for you. Ephesians 2:10, "For we are His workmanship, created in Christ Jesus for good works, which God prepared beforehand that we should walk in them."

Satan tempts us to think poorly of ourselves. Inferiority and low self-esteem keep more people away from a successful life than anything else. Satan knows we can't live any greater than how we think about ourselves. So, if he convinces us we're not worth as much as everyone else around us, we stop believing for things to get any better. Every dream or vision of success we had will be killed. So many of us have quit expecting anything better for our marriage, finances, physical condition or even our walk with God. In fact, we often expect worse things because we don't recognize the effects of our negative thoughts, believing they are true. The reality is; the devil is a liar and a thief. He planted those negative thoughts in our minds so we'll sabotage our own success.

Not knowing who our enemy is and how he works puts us at a disadvantage. Here are some ways that disadvantage works against us:

We see each other as our enemy, not Satan. Yes, he uses people to hurt us, come against us and be stumbling blocks, but it is all part of his covert operations. He is the one who is our real opponent. 1 Peter 5:8 says, "Be sober, be vigilant; because your adversary the devil walks about like a roaring lion, seeking whom he may devour."

We have a wrong perception of our circumstance. Satan is the master of creating circumstances that substantiate the thoughts he placed in our mind. But all circumstances are temporary and changeable. Temporary, because their assignment is limited and will change once we change our mind about them. Don't let your circumstances change you. Instead, change your circumstances by bringing your thoughts into agreement with God's plan for your life, not in agreement with the negative circumstance. Speak God's words instead of the words those circumstances want you to speak.

Knowing your real enemy will dramatically improve your life. Hope and joy will be restored almost immediately and a righteous anger will rise up, giving you a desire to set others free from Satan's deceptions. Let's join together and fight the real enemy—not each other.

▌Learning How to Say No

have observed over the years that when people ask us to do a favor for them, most of us find that it's a lot easier to say yes than it is to say no.

One reason that it's so hard for us to say no is because we are always looking for approval and acceptance from each other. Let's face it; everyone on the face of the earth wants to feel accepted and approved because we don't know how important and valuable we are to God. And because of our blindness to God's love and our personal insecurities, we have a natural tendency to look for people's approval rather than for God's approval.

We have all heard the term, "being a man pleaser". That's what happens when we repeatedly find ourselves saying yes even though we really don't believe in our heart that we should be saying yes. We are just more comfortable saying yes than we are saying no. Sometimes our motive is that we want people to feel that they owe us and we need to control and manipulate them. One of the results of constantly saying yes (when we know that we can't or don't want to do something), is that we end up not fulfilling our word. We find ourselves falling short and letting people down.... in other words we show a lack of integrity.

Lack of integrity becomes part of our legacy, but that's the last thing we want to see happen! Unfortunately the body Christ today is known for its lack of integrity. When you talk to people about their experiences with Christians doing work for them or with some Christian that they were close to at one time, you always hear a common thread. They complain that there is no integrity in the body of Christ. I believe that's because we have never learned to say, no.

I don't mean saying no just for the sake of offending or hurting people. I am talking about saying no when we know in our spirit that it is right. I'm talking about saying no when we know it's what God wants us to do....pleasing Him rather than trying to be a people pleaser. We need the Holy Spirit to help us to discern when to say yes and when to say no. It is easy to operate in human compassion and try to please everybody, but yet it's not God's will and intent that we do that. Let's learn how to respond by being led by the Holy Spirit and not by just our feelings and emotions.

Let's learn how to say no for the right reason so that we can actually bless other people, teaching them to trust in God and not man. God wants to be the one to fulfill their needs and He is the one who should decide how He wants to do that.

Learn to say no when you are being led by the Holy Spirit to say no and, when you do say yes, make sure that it's for the right reasons and motives and that, in the end, it will honor God. When you do agree to do something, make sure that you do whatever it takes to keep your word! Let's once again restore integrity in the body of Christ. Learn how to say, "No."

The Delights of Discipline

Delivered from the Land of "Good Enough"

Too many of us are living far below our God-given potential. We find ourselves stuck in a rut; in our marriages, our life-styles, in our emotions and our spiritual condition, etc.

We have been willing to accept the boundaries set for us by past failures and our present life circumstances. We think we have no control over them and have therefore settled down in "the land of good enough". The desire to move on, increase, excel and advance has left us and we have just accepted the status quo.

In the past I have found myself stuck in a rut concerning the routine of daily life. My sleep patterns, work habits and social life were all stuck in a rut. I had become comfortable living in "the land of good enough" until something happened.

I believe the following points will help you to get out of living in "the land of good enough":

Identify where you are: Getting out of denial is the first step of beginning the process of change. Admit that you are stuck in a rut.

Awaken your spirit: Proverbs 4:23says, "Keep your heart with all diligence, For out of it spring the issues of life." Your spirit is the key to success so allow God to awaken it by stirring up His dreams and His visions in your spirit. Partner with God.

Choose to get out of "the land of good enough" by:

Changing your daily schedule. Do things differently, including the way that you treat people.

Changing your thinking. Write your God-given vision down and re-new your mind with it daily. Habakkuk 2:2-3, "Then the LORD answered me and said: "Write the vision and make it plain on tablets, That he may run who reads it. For the vision is yet for an appointed time; But at the end it will speak, and it will not lie. Though it tarries, wait for it; Because it will surely come, It will not tarry."

Changing your confession. Read God's vision that He revealed to you and then speak it to yourself and others.

Refuse to stay in "the land of good enough". Believe God's promises. Jeremiah 29:11, "For I know the thoughts that I think toward you, says the LORD, thoughts of peace and not of evil, to give you a future and a hope."

Don't Just Believe in His Word. Demonstrate It!

Most Christians know that the will of God is His word and that His word is His will. But we're not supposed to just believe in God's will (word).... We're to demonstrate it! There's a big difference between knowing the right thing to do and actually doing it. Unfortunately, Christians are known for "talking the talk" but rarely known for "walking the walk".

Our job is to show the world a genuine demonstration of who God is and His will for our lives. Romans12:2 says, "And be not conformed to this world: but be ye transformed by the renewing of your mind, that ye may prove what is that good, and acceptable, and perfect, will of God."

Did you catch that? We are to prove the will of God to the world. That proof is exhibited through miracles; the demonstration and manifestation of God's word. Miracles provide irrefutable evidence of God and His will to every human on planet earth.

The Apostle Paul said it this way in 1 Corinthians 2:4," And my speech and my preaching were not with persuasive words of human wisdom, but in demonstration of the Spirit and of power," In other words, he proved that the God he was preaching about was real, by the miracles he performed, not by his eloquent speech.

Like Paul, you can operate in miracles and present the true Bible Jesus to the world. We serve a powerful omnipotent Savior , not a counterfeit religious character with no power to change our lives or circumstances! Here are some points to help you demonstrate God's power.

1. Have a consuming love for God's word. Smith Wigglesworth, the famous man of faith who lived in England in the early 1900's never went more than 15 minutes without reading God's word. Today we label people like him religious fanatics. But, very few people have walked in the miraculous like Smith Wigglesworth.

2. Have an overwhelming confidence in the word of God and the God of the word. Know that He meant what He said and said what He meant. Believe that God's word is the final authority in any given situation. His word cancels everybody else's opinion. God told the prophet Jeremiah that He put His word in his mouth and when Jeremiah declares it, He promises to hasten to perform it.

3. As I just stated, speak, declare and confess God's word. Let God's opinion (the only one that counts) be released concerning your situation. When you say the same thing God says and believe what you say; watch out, a miracle is just about to be manifested!

4. When you've walked out the first 3 steps, step back and keep your mouth shut. When you speak God's word about the circumstance; nothing else is needed. Just "be still and know that He is God". We try to help God by adding words that are often negative, cancelling out what God started. There is an old and true saying, "loose lips sink ships".

Remember, when you speak a lot, there's a greater risk of saying ungodly things, opening the door for Satan. The less said the better, but there is an exception. If you can't hold your tongue, use it to praise God! Keep talking and exalt God with your words, giving Him access to the atmosphere around you. The word says that God inhabits the praises of His people.

Remember, every day the world we live in needs to see the Jesus we love, the real Jesus. Prove His will to them by putting His will on display... demonstrate His word and His will to a lost and dying world!

▌It Takes More than Willpower

Following up on Michele's last blog on habits and addictions; I want you to know that some people are more prone to addictive behaviors than others because of traits passed down through their ancestors or their personalities.

The definition of addiction is: a compulsive overpowering dependency on an object, feeling, or action; habits that cause us to act against our own will. My focus in this blog is to give you some steps to break those controlling addictions in your life.

As stated in the title, will power alone (our inner desires) is not enough. Although God stirs up our willpower to help us desire a breakthrough, there must be a "supporting team" along with our will power to break those addictions and replace them with godly habits.

Get out of denial. Too often we make excuses for repeated bad habits, implying that we have control over them. But we have to admit we are out of control, can't stop it and admit we need help.

Deliverance is necessary. There are no shortcuts to breaking addictions. They are demon spirit-influenced and controlled. The length of time you have had that addiction will dictate the strength of the demonic influence. The good news is there are ministries like Stop Hurting Start Healing that are trained and equipped to help people be set free.

Discover the cause. To every fruit (addictions) there are roots. By researching your history, the way you have been brought up and the traumatic things that occurred in your life, you can discover the root causes of your addictions. Willpower can give you temporary relief, but eventually the cycles of addiction will start over again. Too many of us have given up trying to get free because of this truth.

Replace the bad habits. Certain habit patterns opened the doors to addiction, so replace them with good habit patterns. This takes discipline and a source of accountability. With severe cases of addiction we need other people or programs to intervene in our lives. Joining a healthy-living group like our 3S Program or entering a substance abuse program like the New Life Dream Center are effective tools to help us find the discipline we need to change our current habits and give us the accountability to stay on track.

Give God first place. All addictions come down to idol worship because they have taken the place of the Lordship of Jesus in our life. We depend on them to meet our needs, fill the void in our heart, give us the much needed self-satisfaction, etc. But God needs to be our source, strength and our all in all....nothing else! Jesus tells us in Matthew 6:33 KJV "But seek ye first the kingdom of God, and his righteousness; and all these things shall be added unto you."

Conclusion: Will power is needed and is the first step in the process of breaking addictions (God stirs our desire for a breakthrough). God initiates it, but we have to follow His steps if we want to be free. John 8:36 KJV, "If the Son therefore shall make you free, ye shall be free indeed." You don't have to live your life under demonic influences any longer!

▋ You Lack Just One Thing

When I was talking to God in my quiet time one day, I asked why certain of His promised blessings hadn't come into my life yet. I'm sure many of you have wondered the same thing.

His answer surprised me when He said, "You lack one thing." He brought back to my mind His promise of blessings to Abraham found in Genesis 12:1-3. He said, "Did you notice the very specific instructions I gave Abraham before I pronounced My blessings for his life?"

I read that passage again and found that there were four specific conditions given to Abraham, but he only obeyed three out of the four conditions. The one he didn't obey was the command to leave his nephew Lot behind.

The Lord said, "Abraham only partially obeyed Me and *just one thing* (called Lot) blocked the release of My full blessing in his life." He said to me again in response to my original question, "You lack just one thing!"

God has at times given us a deep conviction to release certain things that hinder our blessing. The problem is that many of us only partially obey and keep "just that one thing" in our lives.

Yes, like Abraham, "the one thing" we hold on to could be blocking our healing, deliverance, marriage restoration or even the financial breakthrough we have been waiting for.

We can even be a worshipper like Abraham or a bible reader or a church-goer, etc.; yet still hang on to "that one thing" (Lot) that's been condemned to the cross.

How can we release God's blessings in our life? Remember He is not holding them back; He wants to bless us. But we are blocking them from being released by our disobedience.

First, be honest about "the one thing" God is pointing out in your life. Be honest about the area of compromise.

Recognize you can't have two landlords over your property (your heart). Make the right choice and allow Jesus to be Lord over your life.

It's dangerous to live in compromise, so separate immediately from "that one thing". Do it NOW!

Don't refuse to listen to the still, small voice of God while it still can be heard.

Don't let a little "Lot" become a big "Lot" like it did in Abraham's life, almost causing him to miss his blessings and his destiny (Genesis 13:7-9).

Finally, remember, you can't train your fleshly desires to be holy so they must be crucified (Galatians 2:20). "The one thing" you are holding onto in your life must be crucified.

CONCLUSION: God loves you and He has already blessed you with everything you need. Remove "that one thing" that God has shown you in your spirit so He can freely bless you. Your destiny depends on it.

▌ Play Now. Pay Later.

There can be no success without the ability to delay gratification and that ability is known as self-control. One of the main reasons our nation is trillions of dollars in debt is that as a society we lack self-control. We reject the idea of having to cut down or do without, so we look for ways to maintain our selfish lifestyle and just let the next generation deal with it. This will be the major factor determining who people vote for in this presidential election.

I believe there are three philosophies of life that drive us as individuals and a society that must be addressed in order to see change.

1. Individualism. This is the root concept of selfishness. It is looking out for number one without any concern for anyone else or the consequences of our actions. Its underlying motive is seeking "what's best for me".... the foundation of the sin nature of every human birthed into this world.

2. Hedonism. The ultimate goal in life is pleasure, if it feels good; do it. It is known in the bible as lawlessness (Matthew 7:21 & 23) " "Not everyone who says to Me, 'Lord, Lord,' shall enter the kingdom of heaven, but he who does the will of My Father in heaven. ....."And then I will declare to them, 'I never knew you; depart from Me, you who practice lawlessness!'" It is single-handedly responsible for most of the moral depravity of our culture today.

3. Minimalism. What I mean by "minimalism" is the philosophy of doing the least yet still expecting the maximum reward. It is the enemy of excellence and the father of mediocrity! I believe this mind-set is responsible for some of our immigration problems and job losses to other nations because things Americans don't want to do are then made available for non-Americans to do. We have gotten lazy and soft and have become a society looking to be served rather than serve; taking the attitude of playing now and paying later. Well the "later" has come and like the proverbial frog in a pot of water that started off cold, we now find ourselves as a nation in hot water.

So what is the solution?

It really is very simple yet we can't do it ourselves....changing the nature of Americans from being, selfish, immoral, lazy, prideful, and pleasure seeking. Our only hope is accepting Jesus Christ as our personal Lord and Savior and living the self-controlled life that He gives us the ability to do.

Changing the nature of an individual ultimately affects society, but can't be accomplished with more education, technology, or even greater wealth. We been there and done that and look where we are today. The true Christians must set the example of what it means to live a Christian life; expressing Jesus' nature. It is a life led by the Holy Spirit; manifesting His fruit in our lives (which includes self-control), preaching the gospel of the kingdom of God and leading people into the saving knowledge of Jesus. This is our only hope. Pay now or pay later. The choice is ours!

Self-Discipline: The Key to a Fulfilled Life

Locked up on the inside of every person, there is untold potential to lead a successful and fulfilled life. The sad story is that most people will never see that potential realized because of this truth... found in just three words.....lack of discipline!

Yes, I believe discipline is the key ingredient in our life that will unlock the greatness that God created in us. What is the simple definition of discipline? It can be summed up in just two words: Delayed gratification! This is the concept of paying now, playing later instead of playing now, paying later.

Discipline means planning long term success by sacrificing instant and short term rewards, because short term rewards eventually lead to long term failure. Most people want discipline, but never achieve it and as a result they're living unfulfilled lives.

There are no short cuts to being disciplined, but these suggestions will help you on your way to a fulfilled life:

1. Schedule the pain. In other words, practice "advanced decision-making". Determine what areas in your life need the most discipline and decide what you're going to do about it. Literally, develop an action plan; that's "advanced decision-making". Don't wait until the last minute every day to make the necessary changes that unlock your great potential.

For example, if you decide your physical condition is the most urgent area in need of discipline, don't wait every morning to decide whether you're going to exercise and eat right that day. Your mind will convince you you're too tired to exercise and it's okay to skip one or two days. But, if it's on your calendar, the decision's already made and you will do it. "Advanced decision-making" helps you to schedule your pain.

2. Practice your discipline. Are your motives for being disciplined right? Do they glorify God and advance His kingdom, or are they selfish reasons?

3. Pre-plan. Don't wait for the last minute. Set at least a six month strategy in place before you start.

Remember, Satan will resist you in your thoughts, because that's where the spiritual war is fought. Discipline starts in your mind first before it can overflow into your actions. Proverbs 23:7a says, "For as he thinks in his heart, so is he.." Reading and memorizing God's word helps you to stay focused in your disciplines. Remember that delayed gratification doesn't mean there's no gratification. The best is yet to come and will eventually keep coming.

4. Be consistent. Many people start, but never finish. So make up your mind to see this discipline through to the end.

5. You don't have to do it alone. Make yourself accountable to others. God created us to be accountable in our relationships so we can support one another in things like discipline. Ask 2-3 people to hold you accountable. Most importantly, depend on the Holy Spirit to help you. He is your Comforter and will give you the encouragement and strength to be disciplined, unlocking the great potential in our life.

The ability to live a fulfilled life is knocking at your door, no matter how young or old you may be. Choose the area that needs the most discipline today and start by taking the second step. By reading this you have already taken your first step!

▌ Seven Times Hotter

here is a sad story I've told many times about a doctor who takes his wife and son on a safari at Kruger Park, South Africa. After an exciting day, they did what they had done the previous nights. They started a camp fire with the intention of adding more wood in the middle of the night to keep the lions away from entering their campsite.

Exhausted from their long day of sightseeing, they fell into a deep sleep and didn't get up in the middle of the night to add more wood to the fire, like they intended. The fire went out and tragedy struck when a lion entered the camp and killed the son as he slept in his tent.

The question I ask is, "Where do lions feed?" The answer is; lions feed where the fire has gone out! The problem with America today is that Satan, the roaring lion, is ravaging our life style and culture. This is happening because the church has lost her fire, passion and hunger for God's tangible presence in her midst. And like a roaring lion, Satan entered into her unprotected camp to wreak havoc in her midst.

The church has lost the cutting edge that's needed to make a difference in today's world. We opted out of the mandate to exhibit a Christ-like lifestyle to influence our culture and instead we've allowed politics and politicians to be the main influence.

We can't expect the government to legislate morality, but we can expect morality to be lived out by the church...role-modeled by those who have been given the nature and power of Jesus Christ. We need to rekindle the fire of our passion and love for God. This fire must burn bright enough to change our culture and keep the lions out of our camp!

What kind of fire am I talking about? I'm talking about the same fire that burned inside the three Hebrew boys; Meshach, Shadrach and Abednego when they refused to bow their knees in worship to the culture they lived in. Because they had that fiery passion, they refused to accept the status quo and were thrown into a fiery furnace that was heated seven times hotter than a normal fire.

Our normal everyday passion for Jesus won't cut it in the gross darkness surrounding us. It must exceed the passion of our weekly "rah, rah" church services; exceed our passion for a new cell phone or updated I-pad and even exceed our misplaced passion for the political leaders we just experienced! Passion for God has to be off the charts!

Let's stoke up the fires of passion seven times greater than we ever experienced before. We can't work it up by ourselves, but God can and I strongly believe He is doing just that right now (and has been for a while).

Face it, our helplessness and weakness to change things in our own strength is evident. We can't stop perfect storms from coming with their devastation; we can't change our culture through political influence, we can't even stop the church's backsliding condition. The only thing that can bring the change that will prepare the way for Jesus' second coming is if our fire of passion is burning seven times hotter!

Let's start praying with abandonment for God's passion to consume us now.... not tomorrow. Let's not leave the upper room until a "suddenly" happens and we recognize God's tangible presence in our midst.

His presence is the only answer to the ills we face today in America. The church has to say, "We will arise and shine for our light has come (Jesus) and the glory of the Lord is risen upon us, (His church). Darkness shall cover the earth, but the Lord will arise over us and His glory will be seen upon us, His church. Remember..... YOU ARE THE CHURCH!

Finding Victory in Christ

▍ Taking Back Control of Your Life

When a person who has offended and hurt you in the past suddenly comes into your presence, how do you react? For many of us, our mood immediately changes and we do everything possible to remove ourselves from their presence.

Past offenses, left undealt-with, make us vulnerable, allowing other people to control our lives. We become slaves to our own feelings and emotions. If we don't break free from pain caused by those past offenses, our history will always show up in our destiny. Living in the past hinders what God planned for our future and also keeps God's present and future blessings on layaway. Every time we react to emotions connected to those past hurts, it's like eating dead things over and over again. Stop it. And release your enemies by forgiving.

The difference between a vulture and humming bird is that a vulture eats things that are dead... They live on what was past. But a humming bird lives on things that have life in them. When you are constantly reminded and controlled by memories from the past, you are eating stuff you ought to be releasing. It won't produce peace or joy. It just weighs you down, like a chicken.

Chickens are earthbound and can only fly a short distance. That's because chickens eat dead things (even their own feces) and are too heavy to soar. In contrast, the eagle flies miles high and only eats things that are alive.

Holding on to offenses does the same thing to us. We lose control of our lives and give it to the person who offended us. It's time to take back control by refusing to internalize what we ought to be releasing! God gave us the ability to purge ourselves from offenses. His nature to forgive has now become our nature as Christians. It's not unusual that the world struggles in this area. They are not equipped like believers in Jesus are. Yet, why do so many Christians struggle as well?

I believe it's because we confuse wickedness with weakness. The person offending us doesn't have to be wicked. Many times they're just weak, unable to resist the temptation that caused them to make a wrong choice. We should all sympathize with that because all of us suffer from time to time with the same weaknesses. The problem is, because we are the victim of their wrong decisions, we consider them wicked and hold onto the offense (and continually eat dead things).

Our unforgiveness doesn't affect them—but us. We want them to pay a heavy price for hurting us, but by dwelling on hurtful memories we are drinking poison. We are "stopped up" spiritually, only hurting ourselves. Just like in our natural body, when we don't release what goes in us, our health is seriously affected.

The solution? Purge yourself by forgiving your offenders. Acknowledge that their weakness is not wickedness. God's word says mercy will triumph over judgment. Sure, your offenders may deserve to be punished, but so do you and I. However, every day God's mercy spares us the just punishment that we rightfully deserve!

Take back control of your life and allow God to bring you into the great destiny He has for you. Stop walking around like a chicken and start soaring like an eagle!

▍ There's No Victory without a Battle

have noticed that most of us have a misconception concerning the way we expect God to comfort us. We are under the impression that God's comfort means either we can totally avoid the uncomfortable issues we face in our daily life, or that He will remove us when we find ourselves in them.

We have concluded that in our walk with God, our main prayer objective is to ask Him to help us avoid all of life's struggles or to release us from the ones we are in. We think that's how God is supposed to comfort us.

But, the root of the word comfort (parakaleo) in the New Testament scripture in 2 Corinthians 1:3&4 means "to call to one's side; to encourage and to strengthen." It never means to make it easy, take care of things for us or remove us from the struggle.

When we read "God of all comfort" it means that God wants to see a number of things accomplished in our life. He is committed to walk with us and encourage us in and through them just like He did with Meshach, Shadrach, and Abed-Nego. When they went into the fiery furnace, they didn't get burnt but they get a greater revelation of who God is!

1. God wants us to know Him better and trust Him more. He uses the struggles we go through to accomplish that. Can you relate to that? I certainly can.

2. Godly character is developed in our lives to increase our influence in the world we live in….many more people would be drawn to Jesus because of us. John 12:32, "And I, if I am lifted up from the earth, will draw all peoples to Myself."

3. When we go through our fiery furnaces with God, we will be prepared to glorify Him as overcomers and be equipped to face our future struggles and battles…leading to future greater victories.

So we need to settle in our hearts that something great will be accomplished in and through the daily struggles we face. It's time to stop asking God to comfort us according to our misconceived notion of comfort. Instead of asking Him to take us out of our struggles we will pray that He comfort us by being with us in the struggles.

Oh yes. I almost forgot to mention another thing.

4. One way God promotes us in His kingdom is through the victories we win from the battles we face.

In other words, the struggle you face is actually proof that God is getting ready to promote you in His kingdom! But, the greater the struggle….the greater the promotion. Wow! I guess some of us are on the verge of great promotions in God's kingdom.

David proves my point. After he faced and killed his Goliath; he was promoted from being a shepherd boy to becoming the king over God's people.

Conclusion: the struggle you face today is about the destiny of tomorrow. The bigger the struggle the more that is at stake. The next time you ask God to comfort you, remember there's no victory without a battle. Don't circumvent your destiny by giving into comfort.

▍ Overcoming the Mountains in Your Life

D o the problems you face seem bigger than life….even bigger than God Himself? Well, I am here to tell you that they aren't! God is infinitely bigger than any problem you have, or ever will have. The question you need to ask is, which is bigger, your God or your mountain? Unfortunately, too many of us would answer that our mountain is bigger.

Our mountains reveal how small and incapable we are to move them out of the way, but they offer an incredible opportunity to discover how great and awesome God really is. Recognize today that your mountain can actually be a blessing in disguise!

The first step to overcome your mountain is to get a fresh revelation of God. Isaiah needed this fresh revelation when he faced his mountain. He faced a leadership crisis in his life and in the nation at the death of King Uzziah. Isaiah 6:1 " In the year that King Uzziah died, I saw the Lord sitting on a throne, high and lifted up, and the train of His robe filled the temple." His discouragement and hopelessness evaporated when God gave him a vision of His greatness, literally changing the prophet's life forever. He now had revelation that, what was impossible for him to overcome, the God he served could overcome.

Understand that God is great and your problem is no match for Him. Get alone with God, with the intention of seeking Him to download a strategy to overcome the mountain you face. Remem-

230 Finding Victory in Christ

ber the advice that the Lord's brother gives us in James 1:5, "If any of you lacks wisdom, let him ask of God, who gives to all liberally and without reproach, and it will be given to him." Keep a pen and paper with you to write down the best four or five possible solutions. Believe that the word God gives you is His strategy to remove your mountain. His promises are true and when applied; they release His power against your mountain.

With humility, prayer and openness to the Holy Spirit, step out in faith to act on one of those solutions. Trust God to close some doors and to open others, unveiling even more possibilities.

Connect with people who are solution-oriented, not with people who just sympathize with you and your problems. There aren't too many visionaries in the world today who see the end from the beginning! Be careful to guard your heart from adopting a victim mentality.

In conclusion, no matter what problems you face, relational, marital, financial, emotional, vocational; you'll find a solution if you have a revelation of how big God truly is. God loves to work with people who know they need His strength. The Lord told the Apostle Paul in 2 Corinthians 12:9a, "And He said to me, "My grace is sufficient for you, for My strength is made perfect in weakness." Don't let yourself be overwhelmed and defeated in life; move your mountain.....you can you know!

▌ Plan to Succeed

This will be a first for me as I share a brief overview of my week with you. If you have been following our blog, you know I've been recommending that we implement new core habits in order to bring positive changes into our life. Well, that is exactly what I did this week, and I have to tell you; I have had a successful week!

One change was to drink a 16oz. bottle of water with natural lemon juice as soon as I got up every morning. Praise God, I was successful for all seven days. I also added stretching to my exercise schedule, which I never did before. As I have gotten older my muscles and joints have shrunk and stiffened up. So I did stretching exercises for my neck, back and legs for about five minutes each day. I already feel the difference when I bend down or turn my neck; activities that had become a little difficult. With just those two additions, a chain reaction started in other areas of my life.

I suggest that you plan how to begin your day even before going to bed because it will impact your todays and your tomorrows. Most of us plan our work times of the day but leave out how we begin our day, which I consider the most important part.

I constantly remind myself why I am alive in this season; why I live where I do and why I have the influence God gave me. This has kept me consistently kingdom-minded, looking for ways to release God's presence everywhere I go and to everyone I meet.

Last week was exceptional. Aside from the opportunity to preach God's word to thousands of people through sermons, face book, bible studies, TV, and radio, I was able to pray for a number of people in a restaurant and a few store owners. One man's back was immediately healed and another man told me a few days later he was delivered from pornography and his hearing was restored. Wow! God is awesome and His mercy endures forever.

It really was a great week in many ways, but in particular because so many of my personal prayers were answered. I'm still learning to not get stressed when problems present themselves. I'm learning to go to God, give them over to him in prayer and stand on His word (which is always the answer to my problem.)

When I remember the track record of God's faithfulness to my prayers, I'm getting less stressed out than I used to. It was a great week and I will be consistent in keeping my core habits, so I expect another great week of living in the supernatural. By the way, I start each day between 4–5:00am except Sunday morning when I start at 3:30am. For me, I do my most important and best work in the morning, but it's important that you find your own rhythm. Of course, I go to bed by 10:00pm whenever possible and most of the time it's earlier. Next time I'll show you how I make use of the 168 hour week that we all have.

Conclusion: We all need to plan to succeed. By not planning daily to succeed means we are planning to fail. Obviously no one on-purpose plans to fail, but we actually do it by not planning to succeed!

▌ Stable in an Unstable World

We live in the most volatile times in mankind's history. Things that were once icons, the pillars and immoveable structures we depended on are literally changing overnight. Long-entrenched governments are toppled within hours, peace is quickly turned into riots and war zones spontaneously erupt. Yet, today's unstable times were prophesied thousands of years ago.

God speaks of a time (I believe we're in that time right now) when people will "call evil good and good evil". At a time like this, people without deep conviction in their beliefs will begin to change their values, standards and way of living.... like the changing of the wind. Our ancestor's beliefs were passed down to us, molded by popular culture and social norms. They are also affected by our intimacy (or lack of intimacy) with God through His word.

Giving in to the pressures of today's worldliness will only lead to instability. Unstable people are not grounded in the truth of the Gospel because it hasn't become the foundation of their life. And, unstable people don't have the anchor of the word to give them a deeper conviction than the inferior and immoral beliefs they're being bombarded with daily. They don't realize that they lack a moral compass, as it says in Matthew 7:13b," wide is the gate and broad is the way that leads to destruction, and there are many who go in by it." In other words, the majority opinion is most often wrong!

On the other hand, people with a biblical world view and strong faith in God are usually stable. They have strong beliefs and aren't vulnerable to the changing morals of the world. Because their lifestyle is established on God's word, unfortunately they're branded as being old-fashioned and out of touch with the times. We can be easily tempted to give in to the pressure and change our belief. But Jesus says in Matthew 5:10&11, "Blessed are those who are persecuted for righteousness sake, for theirs is the kingdom of heaven. Blessed are you when they revile and persecute you, and say all kinds of evil against you falsely for My sake."

The majority opinion today seems to be anti-God and that mindset has crept into the 21st century Christian church. We have developed a compromised gospel to appease the marginal Christian and make friends with the world. Preachers won't speak biblical truth for fear of offending the very people they're called to liberate with God's word. They're more concerned with appearing to be out of step with today's culture than pleasing God.

The fear of the Lord has been replaced with the fear of man, but God is looking for people like us to shout from the roof tops what He has revealed in our hearts. Will the true church (Christlike people) please stand up and be heard? God has not given us a spirit of fear... but of power, love and a sound mind, but it may cost you your life to be stable in this unstable world.

Spiritual warfare is at its highest since the beginning of time because it's Satan's last stand. He is throwing whatever he has left at the church but God is using this season to identify and hand-pick His remnant church to usher in the second coming of Jesus.

Please don't give in...don't give up because of the pressure that this upside down world is throwing at you. keep standing! Ephesians 5:13, "Therefore take up the whole armor of God, that you may be able to withstand in the evil day, and having done all, to stand."

Ask yourself if you're stable in your convictions concerning God's way of life for you? Are you easily swayed by the immoral standards that are intellectually and logically presented to you, even by our government? God is looking for stable people in an unstable world to build his kingdom. What will your choice be?

▌ Step Into Your Miracle

see a great tragedy taking place in the lives of God's people to-day, the tragedy of never discovering their destiny or worse yet.... forfeiting it. Unfortunately, the first generation of Israelites delivered from Egypt also experienced this tragedy. They forfeited their destiny.

The children of Israel were on the brink of their breakthrough miracle as they stood on the shores of the Jordan River. They were about to enter the Promised Land, but instead of stepping into their miracle; their faith failed and they forfeited their destiny; dying before they reached it.

Maybe some of you reading this blog are satisfied with your life; content with what you have, what you do, and what you're experiencing. This message isn't for you. But, some of you won't be denied because you want everything God's promised to you and refuse to settle for less. If that is you.... then keep reading!

There's no victory without a battle and no testimony without a test! The battle isn't directly against Satan; it's a battle of faith (trusting and acting on God's word). James 1:1-3 tells us our faith must be tested. Satan knows the overcoming power of our faith, so he wants us to lose it. 1 John 5:4 says, "For whatever is born of God overcomes the world. And this is the victory that has overcome the world—our faith." If Satan robs our faith, he robs our destiny.

1 Timothy 6:12 says, "fight the good fight of faith and lay hold on eternal life."

Faith is produced when God's word is engrafted and alive in your heart; not just mentally assented to. It becomes the living word that the devil can't steal from you, as described in Mark 4:14, 15. The engrafted word is what keeps you going when you feel like giving up on your God-given destiny. But, every promise from God comes with a price, so remember that the fight isn't about today, but who you'll become tomorrow (your destiny).

I'm certain you bear witness to what I'm saying about the engrafted word. Even if it's a faint bleep on the monitor, identify it and let God re-confirm it, because as you hold on to it, the devil can't rob your destiny. Fight with that word because the weapons of your warfare aren't fleshly. That engrafted word is the two-edged sword God gave you to be used against Satan.

Prophesy your own destiny; it won't happen any other way. Speak (prophecy by declaring the end from the beginning) to the mountain that's in your way. In Matthew 17:20b Jesus says "if you have faith as a mustard seed, you will say to this mountain, 'Move from here to there,' and it will move; and nothing will be impossible for you."

Now, to step into your miracle… in Luke 5:4 Jesus gave Peter the word to launch out. Pater reasoned it, but finally acted upon it and of course he caught a tremendous amount of fish. Step into your miracle by obediently walking out the engrafted word that you're prophesying over your life. Don't make plans to fail, but make plans to succeed by walking out God's word.

Let's go back and see what happened to the second generation of Israelites in Joshua 3:11-17. They followed Joshua's command and as they stepped into the Jordan River, they stepped on the very thing meant to hinder their destiny. The waters of the river withdrew before them and they crossed into the Promised Land on dry ground! They stepped into their miracle because they believed the word that God gave them!

Conclusion: Don't have a "faith failure" and forfeit your destiny. Step into your miracle today.

Good News: The Bad News is Wrong!

God wanted me to tell you something: "The good news is that THE BAD NEWS IS WRONG! Yes, you heard me right! The bad news you heard about yourself, about your destiny and simply accepted as a fact is wrong.

We've been so quick to believe the lies the enemy has spoken about us instead of hanging on to the promises God has given to us. The voice of our circumstance has been shouting louder than the voice of our God-given dreams and visions.

In spite of how it looks, God still holds the promises He redeemed for you. They are not lost or gone forever. They're on God's lay-away plan, waiting for you to claim them once again through your faith. The bill can be paid in full by completely trusting in God's word to you, no matter how long ago He spoke it to you. God's word has a voice and you need to pay more attention to it than natural circumstances that are temporal and changeable.

In Isaiah 53:1 the prophet cried out, "Who has believed our report? And to whom has the arm of the LORD been revealed?" That's the question God still asks today. Your enemy wants you to believe that all is lost and you'll just have to live without the things God promised you.

It's like what the shepherd boy David faced when a lion or bear broke into his sheep fold and carried away a little lamb in his jaws. Well, lions and bears have snatched and killed many lambs before.

What made this different? Let's face it. In such powerful jaws a lamb had no hope, right? Wrong! The good news is THE BAD NEWS IS WRONG!

In spite of seemingly overwhelming circumstances, David rose up, pursued the predator and found that God had prevented the lion's mouth from crushing the fragile lamb. Why? Because the lamb belonged to David! And when David confronted Goliath, he was able to be bold because of what God had taught him through his experience with the lion & bear.

God has given you irrevocable promises concerning things like your marriage, finances, career, job and ministry opportunities, your health, etc. They haven't come to pass yet and it looks like the opportunity to see them fulfilled is over. That's exactly what the lion wants you to believe so you won't pursue them.

The bad news is that they're in the lion's mouth but that news is wrong because the good news is that God didn't allow him to kill your dream and steal what God's redeemed for you. You need to know the good news is......THE BAD NEWS IS WRONG!

In this New Year, take the following simple steps to fully recover what belongs to you, just like David:

Stop feeling sorry for yourself and seeing yourself as a victim of circumstances. You should be in control of your circumstance—not be controlled by them.

Believe God's word, His promises, and acknowledge the integrity of His word. Thank Him for His promises and ask forgiveness for your unbelief.

Stop listening to all the lies and negative voices. Tune in to God's voice of truth instead. Have selective hearing from now on!

Start pursuing your God-given promises by asking for His strategy to recover what's been stolen. His promise for you today is that you'll recover all, but you need to let Him order your steps as you pursue it.

Finally, don't look back. Stay focused on restoring what the devil stole. Constantly remind yourself of this truth: God's good news is THE BAD NEWS IS WRONG!

▌ Don't Take No for an Answer!

Nothing God promises in His word comes without a battle or some kind of warfare; because you see, there's an enemy out there who will do everything he can to block us from receiving the promises. Yet, we can't surrender and live like the bible is just a good story, that it's not real.

Many people today have given up believing that God will keep His word in their life. They've been deceived into thinking it's just not going to happen for them... that the bible is a good holy book with no relevance to their everyday life. Passive Christians are giving into the devil's lies, accepting them as truth over God's word. They accept Satan telling them "No, you can't have this or that from God's word."

We need to develop a war mentality and aggressively refuse to take no for an answer from the devil! Matthew 11:12 says, "And from the days of John the Baptist until now the kingdom of heaven suffers violence, and the violent take it by force." When God says the violent take it by force, He's referring to us.

Jesus was no wimp! He was a mighty warrior, although the weapons of His warfare weren't carnal (like guns and rockets).... His weapons were agape love and forgiveness.

Jesus threw Satan out of heaven to earth, took away his armor and made him a slave, a defeated foe, as are all who have sworn allegiance to him.

242

Jesus is our head, we are His body and He has put all things under His feet. That means as Jesus Christ's ambassador, re-presenting Him on earth, you and I have the same mandate, to keep Satan under our feet.

We just need to remember where His feet are! Well, I'll remind you….. His feet are our feet; so let's get violent against Satan's lies and deceptions. Walk all over him!

For Satan and his demons to triumph over you, you just have to do nothing and stay passive. They count on you accepting defeat, accepting "no", giving up and ultimately quit believing that God's promises will ever come to pass.

Every promise of God has a "yes" to it and an "amen"…. not a no. (Read 2 Corinthians 1:20) God's promises are absolutely yours and He wants you to receive what is rightfully yours.

It's like someone giving you a gift certificate to Macy's, but you never go to claim what is legally yours. The price is already paid; it's just a matter of going to get it. You don't have to beg or try to convince God that you need it. He knew your needs before you existed and supplied all your needs through His grace towards you in Jesus.

Whatever you need today must be violently ripped from Satan's hands through your faith. This is done when you:

1. Believe God's promises are for you right now —not for tomorrow ….but right now! "Faith is now" Hebrews 11:6 tells us, not yesterday or tomorrow.

2. Thank God for what He has already given you even though it hasn't manifested in the natural realm. It's on its way, getting closer and closer as you stay steadfast in your faith.

3. The bible says we need patience and that faith and patience work hand and hand. Our endurance helps us keep believing when Satan sends everything against us to convince us it's not going to happen and it will never happen.

4. Refuse to accept Satan's no! Stay in the battle because God is on your side. He wants the things earmarked for you to get in your hands—not Satan's. Keep declaring the promise and don't waiver no matter what.

This is how to take it by force. Although God meant it for you, you won't get it unless you take it by force. Let's make up our minds to no longer play games with the devil; instead, let's get violent with him! Let's never accept his no as an answer to our God-given promises.

▊ It's Not What it Looks Like

We live in a "two dimensional world", and I believe that not recognizing this truth is responsible for many of life's past, present and future failures. In fact, one dimension controls and dominates the other….. every day.

What am I talking about? The two dimensions I am referring to are the spirit realm and the natural realm. Genesis 1:1, "In the beginning God (Spirit) created the heavens and the earth (natural)."

Although the spirit realm is hidden to the natural eye and is often overlooked, they both coexist and are very real. The forces and influences (good and evil) that affect our everyday life, such as our perceptions, thoughts, attitudes, and passions, flow out of the spirit realm (the unseen realm).

These unseen forces influence our decision-making and consequently our life's destiny. One example of the spirit realm affecting us in a very negative way is when we have a conflict with someone and we get offended and suffer great rejection.

The above scenario can even permanently destroy marriages relationships or close friendships. The extreme conclusion of this negative process can be a raging anger taking control of us and we end up committing the unthinkable…. taking a life!

We can unknowingly become puppets on a string, controlled by this (unseen) spirit realm. Unless we grasp the bigger picture and get the revelation that we live in two dimensions; we will always be victims, not overcomers.

We need to be equipped with the tools to understand the spirit realm and control these forces before they control us and keep us in bondage. This bondage is causing many of us to miss our God-given destinies.

Ephesians 6:12 says " For we do not wrestle against flesh and blood, but against principalities, against powers, against the rulers of the darkness of this age, against spiritual hosts of wickedness in the heavenly places." In other words, our fight isn't in the natural realm against flesh and blood, but it's against spiritual enemies".

So, before we jump to conclusions, we need to stop for a moment and recognize that it's not always what it looks like! Knowing we are in a spiritual battle (but fought in the natural world) is the beginning of a journey to great success. On the flip side; ignorance of this truth will be our demise.

To live victoriously in both worlds simultaneously:

1. Jesus must live in us. His Spirit equips us to deal with the spirit realm successfully. It's not just about going to heaven; it's about defeating the evil forces in the unseen realm.... just like Jesus. Jesus alone makes that possible.

2. We must develop the habit of waiting and listening to God's voice. Psalm 46:10a says "Be still, and know that I am God....." But, unfortunately we are used to making decisions based on what things look like, feel like and what makes sense to us. If we can discern the source of an issue before jumping into life-altering decisions, we can avoid future failure, disaster and bondage.

Remember, every day we're influenced by the spirit realm around us, so it would be good to ask ourselves these questions: Why do I feel this way about this person, my life, my job etc? If I make decisions based on what I feel like now, will it get me closer to God and His destiny for my life? Will it bring long lasting peace and healing in my relationships, etc.? What does God's word say about my circumstances?

Based on our answers to these questions we can determine the source of what we are basing our decisions on. It's not what it looks like, but we can know what it really is by understanding the two dimensions we live in.

In conclusion, the key to success in our relationships, business-es, careers etc, depends on which spiritual force is controlling the decisions we make in the natural world. Remember..... it's not al-ways what it looks like!

▌ Loose Lips Sink Ships!

J ames chapter 3 says that a little rudder can control a huge ship and a small bit in a horse's mouth can control this large and powerful animal. James uses these illustrations to show how the words we speak about our "todays and our tomorrows" will dictate our destiny.

When you consider this privilege, God has given us amazing power over our life and even the world we live in. God created everything by His words and it operates on a word system. Hebrews 1:3a," Who being the brightness of his glory, and the express image of his person, and upholding all things by the word of his power," Hebrews 11:3a, "By faith we understand that the worlds were framed by the word of God,".

Life would be more fulfilling, peaceful and successful if we could have mastery over our words and make sure they line up with God's word. Jesus said in Luke 21:33,"Heaven and earth will pass away, but My words will by no means pass away. "

Let's take a look at how our words affect us and those around us:

1. We say things that hurt people's feelings. We don't recognize the powerful force for good or bad our words have on others as well as on us. We just hurl them without taking thought of the consequences of our words. No wonder we lose friends and people hesitate to be around us. Our words create a friendly or a hostile atmosphere.

2. Today we are the sum total of every word we believed and then spoke over ourselves. There's no getting away from it, our words make us our own worst enemy or our best friend. Instead of finding acceptance by changing our outward appearance through clothes, hairstyles etc. we should try changing our words.

3. Stop undermining the success of your personal relationships and career. You may ask, "How do I do that?" By speaking negative things about yourself to others. So often we knock ourselves, thinking that we're being humble. We don't recognize that it has become a bad habit, negatively impacting our destiny and the way people view us and consequently treat us.

Here's some ways to have better days, be better liked by others and pave the way for a strong and successful ending:

• Don't abuse the privilege of speech. Recognize that the power of speech is a gift from God, so carefully weigh your words before you release them. The consequences of your words can devastate or liberate your future. Proverbs 18:21, "Death and life are in the power of the tongue, and those who love it will eat its fruit." Your words will either curse your life and destiny or will bless you and assure that God's destiny will be fulfilled. Ask yourself this question, "Is Jesus Lord over the words I'm about to speak, or is Satan?

• Satan wages war against you with words. He will do everything he can to get you to curse yourself, because he can't do it. He uses your everyday circumstances to convince you to speak negative words about yourself, others and your future. Instead, speak what God desires for you, especially when everyone else is speaking the complete opposite.

• You need the Holy Spirit. Remember, because you can choose life or death, blessings or curses by your words, you absolutely need the guidance of the Holy Spirit. Trust His warnings and promptings before you speak. Remember...... LOOSE LIPS CAN SINK YOUR SHIP!

Conclusion: Changing your speech pattern will quickly improve everything in your life. By adding just one godly confession about yourself and your destiny every day for one week, you will experience an immediate change. Trust me though; it won't go unchallenged by the devil. He knows the power of your words, but the question today is..... do you? Loose Lips Sink Ships!

How to Become Born Again

The decision to accept Jesus Christ as Lord and Savior is the greatest, most life-changing decision any individual will ever make. Right now, God is waiting with His arms outstretched, for you to turn to Him and receive the new life He offers. The new birth is a simple process. Romans 10:9 says that if you confess with your mouth the Lord Jesus and believe in your heart that God has raised Him from the dead, you will be saved. Pray this prayer:

> Heavenly Father, I realize I am a sinner and I need You in my life. I believe Jesus is the Son of God and that He took my place of punishment by dying on the cross. I ask Jesus to come and live within my heart, to lead me and guide me. I reject satan as my lord and his ways of sin, and I make Jesus Lord of my life. Thank you, God my Father, for accepting me as your child and saving me from eternal torment. I pray this in the Name of Jesus. Amen.

Praise God! Now the next biggest step is to find a church that teaches the uncompromised Word of God. It's essential that you find a place where you can be nourished and encouraged in your new walk. God bless you.

About the Author

Gaspar Anastasi, Apostle of Word of Life Ministries, began this ministry over 34 years ago. In that time, many churches have been planted worldwide under the banner of Word of Life. In 1997 he founded Global Church Fellowship International, a network of churches to train, encourage and support church leaders, particularly in third world countries and inner cities. Twenty-four years ago, Gaspar started an accredited Bible College that even today educates and equips many students in their pursuit of religious studies. In 1983 Pastor Gaspar founded the New Life Dream Centers, a rehabilitation program for drug and alcohol abusers. In the last three decades, this faith-based program has seen thousands of men and women set free from addictions and other dysfunctional lifestyles.

In 2003, Pastor Gaspar & his wife Michele relocated the headquarters for Word of Life Ministries from Freeport, New York to Fort Myers, Florida.

In late 2010, Gaspar established Unlocking Kingdom Destiny, a ministry whose vision is to take back America for Jesus--one city at a time. The ministry's vision is to plant local churches and work with established churches across the U.S. and share the highly successful ministry focus captured by Word Of Life in its 34 years of ministry.

Gaspar and Michele Anastasi host a weekly cable television show called "Stop Hurting Start Healing". Gaspar can also be heard daily on local Christian radio in southwest Florida. His messages can be streamed live on the internet Fridays and Sundays at www.WOLM. net.

Gaspar and Michele have been married more than 46 years and have 5 children and 4 precious grandchildren. They reside in Fort Myers, Florida.

Books by Gaspar Anastasi:

Why Storms Are Good for Your Life

Seven Steps to Complete Forgiveness

God's Answer to Depression

A Light Unto My Path: Daily Meditations to Live By

How to Grow a Church God's Way

Third Day Evangelism

This is War

Discerning the Right Decision

How to Be a Lion Hunter

Freedom from Anger

Stop Hurting Start Healing

Countdown to Your Breakthrough

Finding Lost Love

Get Out of the Land of Good Enough

If you would like to receive one or more of these publications, please write: Word Of Life Ministries, PO Box 60134, Fort Myers, FL 33906 or call 239.244.3912.